unLearning church

church

Just when you
thought you had
leadership
all figured out!

Flagship church resources

from Group Publishing

Innovations From Leading Churches

Flagship Church Resources are your shortcut to innovative and effective leadership ideas. You'll find ideas for every area of church leadership including pastoral ministry, adult ministry, youth ministry, and children's ministry.

Flagship Church Resources are created by the leaders of thriving, dynamic, and trend-setting churches around the country. These nationally recognized teaching churches host regional leadership conferences and are respected by other pastors and church leaders because their approaches to ministry are so effective. These flagship church resources reveal the proven ideas, programs, and principles that these churches have put into practice.

Flagship Church Resources currently available:

- *Doing Life With God*
- *Doing Life With God 2*
- *The Visual Edge:*
  Compelling Video Connectors for Your Worship Experience
- *Mission-Driven Worship:*
  Helping Your Changing Church Celebrate God
- *An Unstoppable Force:*
  Daring to Become the Church God Had in Mind
- *A Follower's Life:*
  12 Group Studies on What It Means to Walk With Jesus
- *Leadership Essentials for Children's Ministry*
- *Keeping Your Head Above Water:*
  Refreshing Insights for Church Leadership
- *Seeing Beyond Church Walls:*
  Action Plans for Touching Your Community
- *unLearning Church:*
  Just When You Thought You Had Leadership All Figured Out!

With more to follow!

Michael Slaughter
with Warren Bird

unLearning church

Just when you thought you had leadership all figured out!

FOREWORD BY LEONARD SWEET

Flagship church resources
from Group Publishing

UnLearning Church

Just when you thought you had leadership all figured out!

CREDITS

Creative Development Editor: Paul Woods
Chief Creative Officer: Joani Schultz
Copy Editor: Lyndsay E. Gerwing
Book Designer: Jean Bruns
Cover Art Director: Jeff A. Storm
Cover Designer: Sarah Gillenwater
Computer Graphic Artist: Stephen Beer
Illustrator: Sarah Gillenwater
Production Manager: Peggy Naylor

LIBRARY OF CONGRESS CATALOGING-IN-PUBLICATION DATA

Slaughter, Michael.
  Unlearning church : just when you thought you had leadership all figured out! / by
  Michael Slaughter with Warren Bird.
    p .cm.
  Includes bibliographical references.
  ISBN 0-7644-2297-9
    1. Christian leadership. I. Bird, Warren. II. Title.

  BV652.1 .S585 2001
  259--dc21

                                2001054514

10 9 8 7 6 5 4 3 2 1   11 10 09 08 07 06 05 04 03 02

Printed in the United States of America.

Contents

SECTION 1
UnLearning Church:
A High-Touch Experience of God in a High-Tech World

SECTION 2

UnLearning LeaderShip:

SECTION 3

UnLearning Life:

Authentic Demonstrations of Kingdom Living

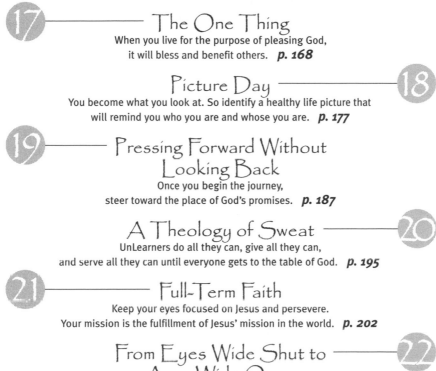

dedication

I dedicate this book to my parents,
Nolan and Bettye Slaughter,
who by faith gave me to God
and raised me in Christ's church.

owledgments

This book was a team effort.

Warren Bird and I dialogued regularly by phone through numerous ideas and drafts. We talked and prayed together from my summer sabbatical to my fall heart scare, through winter snow days and into 2001. Each week I'd tell him that the most important idea in the book was the idea that God is doing a new thing with the next generation of leaders and churches. I am grateful to **this emerging generation of church leaders** who are anchored both in the ancient truths of Scripture and in an atmosphere of innovation and change.

My life companion of more than twenty years, **Carolyn Slaughter,** has experienced the realities of *unLearning Church* more than anyone else. I can't voice high enough tribute for her friendship, love, and demonstration of authentic faith. Our children, **Kristen** and **Jonathan,** have once again graciously given permission for many family moments to become teaching events in this book.

Ginghamsburg's worship design team meets with me each week, and many of their creative insights have significantly shaped this book. I thank God for the influence of each of them. The design team includes creative director **Kim Miller,** who has dreamed many of the concepts with me and developed many of the illustrations used first in worship celebrations or conference presentations and then again in this book. The design team also has included **Todd Carter, Chris Gates, Brent Thurston, Fran Wyatt, Tom Lipps,** and **Carolyn Slaughter.**

Several people on staff at Ginghamsburg have brainstormed with me on the title and subtitle, critiqued the look and feel of sample chapters, and suggested improvements on the actual wording as the book moved from outline to final draft. These include Carolyn and Kim on the above-mentioned design team. **Kate Johnsen, Tammy Kelley, Sherry Douglas,** and **Sue Nilson** have also provided feedback.

Office assistants **Penny Powers, Gerry Pass, Brenda Denney, Laura Glazier,** and **Denise James** were a great help, along with numerous others in the church office.

Ginghamsburg's cyberteams serve a far larger congregation than Ginghamsburg does on premises. This hardworking group places video, audio, and printable versions of our weekly teachings on our Web site, www.ginghamsburg.org. They also include a devotional guide online. Under the leadership of **Mark Stephenson,** each month they help literally thousands of people from around the globe. As a side benefit, their background work greatly assisted the editorial process of this book. Besides Mark, some of the most heavily involved members of the CyberMinistry sermon teams are **Jerry Warner, Steve Curtis, Pamela Neveu, Angie Goldsboro, Pat Hedleston, Pam McHone, Patrice Mumpower, Karen Wendt, Linda Dean, Carolyn Slaughter,** and **Sheila West.** Most are unpaid servants of Jesus Christ.

Several of my mentors and colleagues in ministry took time to offer comments on a draft of the book. They include **Bart Campolo, Janet L. Dale, Troy Dean, Harvey Ignacio, Jack Jackson, Erwin McManus, Karen Medlin, Jessica Moffatt, David Olshine, Nancy Burgin Rankin, Len Sweet, Dick Wills, Jodi Clegg,** and **Lisa Lakatos.**

Finally I want to thank our friends at Group Publishing. **Thom and Joani Schultz** took time to come to Ohio to meet with Carolyn and me. Several key staff members from Group have visited Ginghamsburg. **Paul Woods,** as creative development editor and acquisition editor for the flagship church line, has patiently kept us on focus.

I thank **God** for all these brothers and sisters who walk with me and who cheer me on, even as I cheer them on. We take responsibility in **Jesus Christ** to climb on, higher and upward, as we focus toward God's irresistible future.

foreword

Don't Take It From Mike

I came of age in a world that believed in "experts."

I grew up in an academic world that actually believed that scholarship and scientific knowledge could solve all the problems of the world: poverty, racism, crime, etc. Just do good enough research, get all the facts together, write a paper that uses the scientific method to formulate a solution, submit the formula to peer review, and...

Presto! Problem solved.

Adolph Hitler called this the "rule of experts" or "*Fuhrerprinzip,*" which literally means the right of superior minds to unquestioning obedience and special treatment.

Fuhrerprinzip is finished. What killed the "rule of experts"? First, the solutions that "experts" came up with often made the problems worse and/or created new problems.

Second, experts lied and lost trust. Two examples: In spite of reassurances from health experts and governmental sources, (a) eating contaminated beef really could cause "Mad Cow Disease" (BSE), and (b) the combined MMR vaccine in Britain is now linked to a growing incidence of bowel disease and autism.

Third, scientific studies themselves demonstrate that the "common people," when given the right information and time to make conclusions, are "wiser" on social policy issues than social scientists and other "experts."

That's why I often begin my presentations with the disclaimer "Don't take it from me."

In the modern world, "experts" asked us to "Take it from me."

Forget it. Don't take it from me. I boast no immaculate perceptions. Like everyone else, I see "through a glass, dimly." I know only "in part." All perception is

smudged. There is in my life a large element of not-knowing.

I know just enough to know that I don't know as much as I should know. The people to fear are those who don't know enough to know that they don't know. Willard Quine, who some claim was the most important philosopher of the second half of the 20th century, took all the "?" keys off his typewriters. He quipped that he didn't need them because he dealt in certainties.

Really, Mr. Quine!

I am like the seminary professor with the "80/20 rule": He claimed that 80 percent of his theology was right and 20 percent was wrong. He just didn't know which was which. I don't even agree with myself and some of the things I wrote ten years ago. Don't believe what I say because you believe me. You must know inside yourself that what I'm saying is true. All I'm doing is giving you a template for you to test your own experiences and observations.

One person paid me the ultimate compliment: "Dr. Sweet, this is the fourth time I've heard you. You certainly are interesting. But I'm going to tell you something. You never tell me anything I don't already know, but until you say it I don't know I know it."

Don't take it from me.

If what I'm saying doesn't ring true in your soul or ring a bell in your brain, I could be wrong. That could be my 20 percent. Of course, that could also be your 20 percent. Either way, we need to check each other and test the Spirit.

Don't take it from Mike Slaughter either.

If you don't already know inside that what Mike is saying is true...

If, as you're reading what follows, you aren't saying, "Hey, I already knew that—I just didn't have words for it..."

If Mike is not saying things here that you've already felt deep inside but not brought to consciousness...

If this book doesn't illuminate what you think but didn't know you thought until you read it here...

Then don't take it from Mike.

But if, as you read this book, you find yourself saying over and over again, as I did, "Oh, I see...I see..."

If God is giving us flashes of insight: "Aha...Amen..."

If God is opening in us an awareness of "that's right...of course..."

Then we're not taking it from Mike.

We're taking it from the Spirit.

The Holy Spirit is resonating with both our spirits and Mike's spirit to move us from belief to faith, from "ought" and "should" to "must." Besides, as Mike is the first to tell us, it's not about him anyway. It's all about Jesus and his "must" claims in our life.

unLearning Church is a "must" book for church leaders.

Leonard Sweet

E. Stanley Jones Professor of Evangelism
Drew Theological School
Madison, New Jersey
www.LeonardSweet.com

introductio

Time to unLearn

A friend who is under thirty-five told me this story of a major transition that happened in his life and ministry:

When God began to nudge my wife and me toward starting a church, I began looking for someone who was "doing church right." I had grown up in churches that pushed me to participate in worship and ministry but in which very few people actually met Jesus and became a part of those communities.

My search led me to attend a conference at a well-known teaching church. I was so inspired about reaching lost people that I remember crying with joy intermittently through many of the talks. My wife and I set out to plant a church just like the one I had visited. At conference time the next year, I brought all our key people from the new congregation we were launching in Clemson, South Carolina. We each left the conference ready to build that church in our state.

IT TOOK US ABOUT six months
TO REALIZE THAT SOMETHING WAS
seriously wrong.

It wasn't working, our generation wasn't responding, and I felt like quitting. It was as if we were putting on a big performance that left people unaffected.

Fortunately, God is faithful and taught us in our discouragement. He used the teaching church to free me to be creative and think outside the box and inside the Spirit's leading. God took that freedom and many of the things I had been taught growing up about a more participative church and blended them into something that appealed to and changed Clemson students.

WE MADE A BUNCH OF CHANGES
ALL AT ONCE, AND LIVES BEGAN TO
turn toward Jesus.

We moved from a school auditorium to a bar, from morning gatherings to night gatherings, and from lousy music to a solid worship band.

More important, what really changed us and the course of the church was our move to make high-engagement worship central to everything we did. We became worshippers and a real family. We began to build a faith community that experienced worship, a sense of family, and personal growth. The church expanded rapidly toward God and numerically over the next three years.

—John Reeves

unLearning Church is about people like John. I hope it is also about people like you.

The following pages address the unique qualities of *your* church, *your* community, *your* leadership, and *your* life. This book is about leaders in churches, old and young, daring to leave the status quo and fearlessly stepping out into God's promising and yet unknown future. It's about "unLearners" on the cutting edge of how God works best: through unique personalities localized to their context. It's about the prophetic witness to Christ's presence in individual communities with a ripple effect reaching around the world.

No longer can any one community of Christ's followers dictate what another church must do to succeed. I'm "unLearning" the model of cloning someone else's blueprint. That era is over.

GOD'S KINGDOM IS not BEST REPRESENTED BY FRANCHISES OF McChurch.

If you focus your energies on copying someone else's methodologies or programs, you will miss something crucially important.

If you'll not uncover a franchise model in these pages, then what will you find?

THE HOLY SPIRIT IS EMPOWERING transformational leaders WHO DEMONSTRATE THE KINGDOM OF GOD IN UNIQUE WAYS IN EACH DIFFERENT COMMUNITY.

That's a world of difference from copying someone else's ministry and building a "been there, done that, bought the T-shirt" look-alike.

Every church leader has a specific call and distinguishing gift base of talent. You already have the God-given gifts you need. Your mission is to use them to excel in a local implementation of the overall mission of Jesus Christ. Your effectiveness in the future will be measured by how well your church demonstrates the kingdom of God in unique ways to your indigenous community and beyond. Your goal is to connect people to an authentic experience of God in this world.

AN ANCIENT-FUTURE ANSWER

Today's emerging churches are anchoring themselves in the ancient truths of biblical authority, yet they're operating in an atmosphere of innovation and change. Armed with a strong sense of "first causes," they're forming distinctive communities of faith. They are safe spaces for spiritually hungry hearts, environments of deep connection, experiences of community, and centers of involvement in the pursuit of social justice.

The surrounding culture has significantly changed in recent years.

THIS BOOK IS AN URGENT CALL FOR
spiritual and prophetic leadership
TOWARD THE NEW DEVELOPMENTS IN OUR CULTURE.

The question is not "What is Ginghamsburg (or *Pick-Your-Favorite* Church) doing these days?" Nor is the motivation to climb the American ladder named bigger-better-more.

The call is to unLearn—
TO BREAK THE RULES OF CONVENTIONAL WISDOM

IN ORDER TO TRANSLATE GOD'S ANCIENT PURPOSES

TO TODAY'S POSTMODERN WORLD.

The challenge is to translate and target those purposes to each indigenous environment.

THIS BOOK IS ABOUT VISUALIZING AND ARTICULATING
alternative pathways of ministry
BASED ON WHO YOU ARE AND HOW GOD HAS UNIQUELY GIFTED YOU.

It addresses the fulfillment of your life mission as a church leader, your specific commitment to spiritual growth, and your ministry focus for the next year.

The section dividers provide a framework for the journey. They forecast three areas of unLearning. Through each one, you can create environments in which people can become radical followers of Jesus Christ:

Section 1 shows how unLearning CHURCHES connect people with a high-touch experience of God in a high-tech world.

Section 2 shows how unLearning LEADERSHIP empowers servants of God to do the mission of Jesus.

Section 3 shows how your unLearning LIFE creates an authentic demonstration of kingdom living.

Each section challenges you to name where you want to go. What does the next step look like? Jeremiah the prophet was painting a picture of a promising future, and God asked, "What do you see?" (Jeremiah 1:11, 13).

RADICAL ABANDONMENT AND EVANGELISM

The three sections are not about continuing what you are already doing: simply slapping on a new slogan, better technology, or some other additive. The goal of this book is not to showcase the latest program or to give you a numbered list of how-to steps.

The challenge in these pages is to hear and obey God with a sense of radical abandonment. The result will be new ways of ministering to people, using the resources God has already given to you.

Radical abandonment to Jesus is much more holistic than it is prescriptive formulas.

JESUS ROSE FROM THE GRAVE, LOOKED AT HIS DISCIPLES, AND SAID,
"You will receive power" (ACTS 1:8).

A revolutionary power. An uncommon power. Power to be witnesses in the power of the Holy Spirit.

The challenge is to find and follow God's directive *for you*. Your local implementation may take on a one-of-a-kind flavor seen nowhere else. (See page 18 for two examples.) Yet the results will be similar: You'll design communities invaded by the presence of God through Jesus Christ that demonstrate the very kingdom of God. Radical Christianity is being the hands and feet of Jesus Christ, led and empowered by the Holy Spirit, ready to serve and give witness whenever and to whomever God calls us to reach, in ways uniquely appropriate for each particular community.

IT'S TIME TO GO BEYOND KNOWING AND BELIEVING GOD'S TRUTH TO EXPERIENCING AND demonstrating God's presence.

God wants you to be authentic, the real deal, becoming a change agent for the entire world.

each church finds its own flavor

Everything about Princeton Alliance Church at the Crossroads says, "Urban professionals are welcome here." The church campus in New Jersey's research corridor was intentionally constructed to look like the executive office parks nearby. Each church ministry models a quality standard consistent with the surrounding business community.

Not surprisingly, the church has made great inroads for Christ with executives and managers at nearby Merrill Lynch, Bloomberg, and Bristol-Myers Squibb. "Our calling is to reach everyone we can," says senior pastor Bob Cushman, "but we know we're best at connecting with urban professionals, so that's why we build a corporate feel into all we do."

Six hundred miles to the southwest, Quest Community Church in Lexington, Kentucky, has a similar passion for outreach but does best at impacting a different community. Pastor Pete Hise is proud of the fact that 25 percent of the people who attend Sunday mornings are either atheists or agnostics. He's particularly glad that young people with body piercings find lots of others at the church who look like them. "Which church in Lexington will reach that kind of person for Jesus?" he asks. "The one gaping hole in most churches' ministry is in reaching the Generation X crowd. That's what we do best." He estimates that as many as 300,000 people in greater Lexington need to hear about Jesus in a way they have not yet heard.

These two churches share the same overall mission of turning irreligious people into committed followers of Christ, but the local expressions are completely different. Each is appropriate for some segment of its community. Each of these churches has found its own flavor.

START BY UNLEARNING

To become an indigenous, relevant community, you will unLearn lots of things you thought were right.

UnLearning is about going a different direction. UnLearning means repentance. It requires us to identify ways we were wrong and to rebuild in a new direction.

UnLearning may mean you have to leave the group because a crowd will always be slower to respond to the voice of Jesus Christ. If you always follow the pack, you will miss the miracle moment for which you were created.

UnLearning is about ways the Holy Spirit can adjust your leadership skills and attitudes. Then you, in turn, can lead the way for a similar transformation in others.

LEADERS WHO UNLEARN ARE
a different breed
FROM WHAT YOU MAY BE USED TO.

They are willing to fail. They break their own rules—at least the rules that prohibit people from becoming passionate followers of Jesus.

UnLearning churches demonstrate an uncompromising approach to church mission and ministry. It may seem new, but it's actually an ancient approach.

Why a book about *unLearning*? Any navigator who travels fluid waters knows the need to change the angle of a boat's sails as soon as the wind blows from a new direction. Today's ocean of constantly changing pop-culture breezes may make you uncomfortable. I hope this book challenges you, as well, and even makes you feel a bit uneasy. Discomfort precedes change.

Tension spurs learning and growth. It's important for you to ask questions that other leaders may not be asking. Now is the time to seriously evaluate what you're doing in light of the fresh wind of God's Spirit blowing through a post-Christian world.

Most important, unLearning is about experience.

UNLEARNING CHURCH WILL INSPIRE YOU
TO CREATE SAFE SPACE, AN ENVIRONMENT IN WHICH
PEOPLE ARE FREE TO BECOME
radical followers of
Jesus Christ.

This book will challenge how you see and do church. It will speak to both head and heart, and chances are you'll find yourself on an unexpected spiritual journey.

Are you ready to take yourself and your church on that kind of journey? Ready to unLearn anything in your church, leadership, or lifestyle that stands in the way?

GOD IS CALLING PEOPLE TO DEVELOP FAITH COMMUNITIES THAT
EFFECTIVELY REACH UNCHURCHED POPULATIONS FOR JESUS CHRIST
IN A POSTMODERN, POST-CHRISTIAN WORLD—
RADICAL DISCIPLES abandoned to
the purpose of evangelism.

Want to be there? Then let's begin unLearning.

unLearning church

A High-Touch Experience of God in a High-Tech World

Born to Be Wild

UnLearning churches defy old identities. They don't fit into the usual categories. They're tough to label, difficult to classify, and downright unpredictable. The people at the helm are fully dependent on the leading of the unseen Spirit of God.

"Church growth" was the mantra of the 1980s and 1990s. I attended my first "Breaking the Two Hundred Barrier" conference shortly after becoming Ginghamsburg's pastor. Then I enrolled in "Breaking Four Hundred" and "Breaking Eight Hundred."

We became experts at methodologies that involved small group and Sunday school ministries. We shifted from a programmatic approach to a cell-driven approach. We began to develop associations around the successful megachurches of that day. We learned about the pastor as CEO, and I adopted that model.

TO MOVE FORWARD I HAVE HAD TO unLearn the megachurch and CEO model.

If we continue to copy the models of the 1980s and 1990s, we're going to miss the next generation. I'm now learning to take my cues from the age group that's under thirty-five.

As recently as three years ago, I thought the contemporary megachurch would be the church of the future. It was the kind of church almost everyone seemed to aspire to become. Our culture preferred Wal-Mart superstores to the corner drugstore and giant Home Depots to local hardware stores. It made sense for churches to follow the same pattern.

Change is so constant today that no one can predict the effective church of the future, yet I don't believe it will be the shopping-mall-size megachurch. As many growing churches have demonstrated, once you exceed an attendance of four hundred, a majority of growth can be transfer growth from already-churched populations. Some megachurches have seen success in reaching unchurched populations, but too often church growth in the United States and Canada does not represent net gains for the kingdom of God.

A one-size-fits-all approach TOWARD GROWTH WILL definitely not BE THE MOST EFFECTIVE MODEL OF THE TWENTY-FIRST CENTURY.

A seismic shift is occurring in the practice of church. Emerging churches are defying many of the formulas of the late twentieth-century church growth movement. They don't fit into just one category, such as the much-publicized phenomenon known as the megachurch movement.

The newest islands of health and hope are not the "Fortune 500 churches"— the established models of the 80s and 90s that everyone was trying to clone.

A NEW "DOT-COM-STYLE" GROUP OF unique churches IS EMERGING.

These dot-com churches, led by a new breed of young innovators, noticeably resist trying to duplicate the successful church-growth models of the last century.

I recently visited five effective "dot-com" churches in Oklahoma City, each with one thousand or more in attendance, but they're all growing in ways different from one another. They are not all trying to look like the same model. One church emphasizes the Creation. Its campus is full of waterfalls and living plants, and it sponsors a wide diversity of life-generating ministries in the community, from an eye clinic in the inner city to programs for ex-offenders. Another communicates the atmosphere of a high-class hotel, building a more classical atmosphere and reaching the upper-middle-class with strong ministries to singles and blended-families.*

Churches like these are as different from the Fortune 500 group as the new e-commerce industries are from brick-and-mortar operations like General Motors, Coca-Cola, and Procter & Gamble. Their distinctiveness goes far beyond denominational differences and worship styles.

In fact, these unLearning churches defy many of the old descriptive labels. They could not be photographed for a look-alike contest. They can't be traced to

---

*For three of the better examples see United Methodist Church of the Servant, www.umcservant .org/main.htm; Life Church, www.lifechurchokc.org; and Crossings Community Church (formerly known as Belle Isle Community Church), www.crossingsokc.org.

the same cookie-cutter mold.

Their commonality is that they excel in local implementation. They connect people in their communities or cultures to an experience of God, to authentic community, and to life purpose. They're radically local within the same cities but reaching distinctly different people groups.

If the emerging church IS RECOGNIZED AND VALUED FOR ANYTHING, IT'S FOR A HIGHLY EFFECTIVE, INDIGENOUS CARRYING OUT OF the mission of Jesus Christ.

This next generation of churches goes far beyond a simple name change from "Methodist" or "Baptist" to "Community Church" or "Neighborhood Church." That trend was perhaps the first sign of the more indigenous focus evident today.

UnLearning churches resist the usual CATEGORIES.

They blow off such identities as traditional or contemporary; evangelical or liberal; large or small; suburban, urban, or rural; and even Catholic or Protestant. They don't fit neatly into categorized boxes.

EACH OF THEIR HEARTS IS TO uniquely demonstrate THE PRESENCE OF GOD IN THEIR OWN NATIVE SETTINGS.

PATRON SAINTS OF UNLEARNING

Think about the Christmas story, especially the unprecedented, supernatural way Mary became pregnant. If you were Joseph, shocked to hear that your fiancée Mary had a baby in her womb, would you believe the dream in which an angel of the Lord appeared to you? The angel said, "Joseph, son of David, do not be afraid to take Mary as your wife, for the child conceived in her is from the Holy Spirit" (Matthew 1:20).

Everything within Joseph told him that the best thing to do would be to divorce Mary quietly. Instead he acted on an intuitive sense of the Spirit. He took a huge risk in how he followed God.

That's what unLearning leaders are helping other people do.

Anybody God uses

TO ACCOMPLISH A MIRACULOUS PURPOSE

takes risks and dreams

OUT OF THIS INTUITIVE VOICE OF THE SPIRIT THAT CALLS WITHIN.

The idea behind this book was birthed in a way similar to Peter's experience in the middle of the Sea of Galilee. The disciples, riding in a small boat, battling fierce waves and winds, saw Jesus walking calmly across the water. They were all terrified.

In all their panic of going against the wind, the disciples forgot that Jesus would not be distant and uninvolved. Jesus was right there with them, walking on the water.

Yet most of them couldn't recognize him. They thought he was a ghost.

Peter, on the other hand, got out of the boat and walked on the water because his faith told him that it was Jesus out there. "But when he noticed the strong wind, he became frightened, and beginning to sink, he cried out, 'Lord, save me!' Jesus immediately reached out his hand and caught him, saying to him, 'You of little faith, why did you doubt?'" (Matthew 14:30-31).

Peter was the only one who risked. He chose to block out the voice of the storm. Instead, he focused on Jesus, who said, "Come."

PETER DID THE IMPOSSIBLE

BECAUSE HE RESPONDED TO

the voice of Jesus INSTEAD OF LISTENING

TO THE STORMS AND THE FEARS OF OTHERS.

Peter didn't begin to experience problems until he began to pay attention to the raging water through his physical eyes. He got in trouble when he began to look at the raging storm rather than look into the eyes of the one who had said, "Follow me" (Matthew 4:19).

STILL LISTENING TODAY

UnLearning leaders listen to God through more than their cognitive minds. God also speaks to hearts in the form of the Holy Spirit. When you begin to sense in your heart that Jesus Christ is continually with you, then you can risk and step out to obey God in new and adventurous ways.

That same risk-taking shows up in people throughout history, in all fields of life. Imagine, for example, growing up in eighteenth-century Europe, where slavery was a long-established, virtually unchallenged tradition. Everyone around you said that slavery is normal, natural, unavoidable, and perhaps even necessary. Yet a Christian named William Wilberforce saw the unseen and took a faith risk. In 1789 he led a campaign against the British slave trade. He continued to champion the impossible. In 1807 the impossible happened: Great Britain abolished slavery in the British colonies. In 1833 an act of Parliament called for the abolition of slavery throughout the British Empire.

Here in the United States, a man named Millard Fuller believed he could change the face of housing for the poor in America. He founded an organization called Habitat for Humanity, which has built more than 100,000 homes around the world for people in need—all "because of Jesus," he says. "We are putting God's love into action."[1]

Even our fantasy world applauds the idea of taking risks to do the impossible. In the movie *Indiana Jones and the Last Crusade*, Indiana steps out onto a bridge that isn't yet there, or at least doesn't seem to be there. Instead of falling to his death, however, he rests his foot on something solid but heretofore unseen.

If you watch life through human perception alone, and if you listen only to the fury of the storm, you'll stop, paralyzed with fear. When the Holy Spirit in you develops a heart-based relationship with God, you listen with the ears of your heart and see through the eyes of your heart. That's when miracles happen.

Pastoral ministry has taught me much about this process. When I went to seminary, I learned that church services are about preaching, music, and prayer. But I saw pictures through the eyes of my heart. I saw a church marked by visual media and music with an edge. I envisioned a way to communicate God's love to ordinary people like me who didn't connect with church the way church was being done in most places.

NEW MEANING FOR FAILURE

Peter was not a failure because he looked down and began to sink.

IF ANYONE FAILED,
IT WAS THE ELEVEN WHO stayed in the boat,
WAITING TO SEE IF IT COULD BE DONE.

The church I've served for more than twenty years is simply a representation of what God is willing to do in ordinary places, when commonplace people are willing to follow the voice of God and step out of the boat, just like Peter did.

This book is certainly not a prescriptive laundry list describing how to replicate Mike Slaughter's ministry at Ginghamsburg. I've made more mistakes than I care to remember. I wrongly bought into the pastor-as-CEO model during the 1990s and forgot that I am to be a spiritual guide and coach. We grew from an attendance of 1,200 to over 3,000 in four years, but much of the growth lacked a depth of spiritual maturity. As a result, the more we grew numerically, the more we watered down our commitment to radical discipleship.

Our breakthroughs are certainly not because Ginghamsburg has a brilliant leader. My wife and best friend, Carolyn, often reminds me that if God could speak through Balaam's ass (see Numbers 22:28-35), God can also speak through me! As she well knows, my high school transcript is covered with Cs, Ds, and Fs. *Mediocre* is too generous a word for it.

I made it through college, seminary, and a doctorate, but I still cannot find anyone who thinks Mike Slaughter has it all figured out. Every week I still receive letters from people in the congregation who tell me ways we could do things better. Every week there's the possibility that someone will get ticked and leave.

I am simply the person who God has called me to be. Every day I pray, following the example of Paul in Philippians 3, "Lord, I don't want to play church. Use me for your purpose. I want to know the power of your Resurrection and the fellowship of your suffering."

RESURRECTION POWER

Jesus, after the Resurrection, warned his followers not to go out alone. He told them to "wait there for the promise of the Father" when they would "be baptized with the Holy Spirit" (Acts 1:4-5).

Think about the implications. Jesus' followers had been with him for three years. (That's a whole lot better than attending a weeklong church growth conference.) Didn't they learn enough about Jesus by watching and copying his work?

JESUS CLAIMED THAT

information and imitation

ARE NOT ENOUGH.

He told his followers, in effect, "Don't go out there and attempt this until you have encountered the invading power of God in your life, for until you encounter the resurrected Christ, all you'll have is information. You will never have the experience or the power." (See Acts 1:4-8.)

I remember one of my first encounters with God. It seemed like God was chasing me. It was the summer of 1967, and I was at a real low point in my life. Two of my friends had just been busted for drugs. My mom and dad were frustrated with me. They decided to send me down south to visit relatives I had never met. They wanted to "keep me in touch with my roots," they said.

During that time I would lie, cheat, or do anything to get what I wanted. I even had some help at breaking the rules. A few days before graduation from high school, one teacher changed an F to a D so I could graduate. In another class I copied off of someone else's exam so I could pass. I had no interest in doing things in ways that pleased God.

Yet God was chasing me, and these God-whispers would pop up everywhere I went. In fact, all these God-whispers troubled me so much that I remember calling my girlfriend long-distance to talk about it.

God had never bothered me like this before. God even went ahead of me into the restroom of a two-pump gas station in the backwaters of rural Arkansas. There, scrawled on the wall above the urinal, were these words: "Jesus saves all who want him."

The outcome of this experience and others in the ensuing months was life-changing.

I TRULY ENCOUNTERED THE RESURRECTED JESUS CHRIST, WHICH ultimately changed everything.

JESUS SAVED ME, AND I WANTED HIM.

Many Christians today wear bracelets with the letters WWJD. These bracelets are designed to help us ask ourselves, "What would Jesus do?" The idea is to try to determine what Jesus would do in a situation and then to imitate Jesus' response.

But imitation is not enough.

Living for God

IS NOT IMITATION; IT INVOLVES CRUCIFIXION.

The Bible says in Galatians 2:19b-20, "I have been crucified with Christ; and it is no longer I who live, but it is Christ who lives in me. And the life I now live in the flesh I live by faith in the Son of God, who loved me and gave himself for me."

Jesus moved into my life, changing my priorities, my values, and my relationships. He transformed everything in my life.

"Christ in me" is the source of resurrection power. It comes only through my being dead, buried, and out of the way. When we say "yes" to Jesus, we are "buried with him by baptism into death, so that, just as Christ was raised from the dead by the glory of the Father, so we too might walk in newness of life" (Romans 6:4).

CALLED TO SERVE

God has chosen you, called you, gifted you, and promised a fulfillment of your life mission.

GOD WOULD NOT CREATE YOU FOR failure.

Your success is based on your willingness to risk stepping out and to obediently follow God. All of us experience seasons of doubt and frustration;

UNLEARNING LEADERS step out of the boat ANYWAY.

My encounter with Jesus Christ in my late teens was revolutionary. From that time forward, I knew I wanted to reach a target population that has been turned off or out by the established church. This group represents a huge number of people. On any given weekend, up to three-quarters of Americans[2]—and an even higher number of Canadians[3]—are not in church. Those are the people I want to reach. I'm thankful for congregations that nurture the already churched, but I'm interested in finding ways to speak to the unchurched.

I WANT TO invest my life IN THOSE WHO WANT TO PURSUE RADICAL CHRISTIANITY.

The emerging leader is not enamored with the latest religion of self-actualization. The religion of talk-show television is a rudderless spirituality. Jesus calls us to self-expenditure, not self-infatuation. He says, "If any want to become my followers, let them deny themselves and take up their cross daily and follow me. For those who want to save their life will lose it, and those who lose their life for my sake will save it" (Luke 9:23-24).

I don't want TO LEAD A MEGACHURCH OF PEOPLE WHO COME TOGETHER TO BE INSPIRED TO LIVE status-quo lives PEPPERED WITH JUDEO-CHRISTIAN VALUES.

I want to empower radical followers of Jesus.

Followers of Christ have a rudder that goes deep into the ways of God as revealed in Scripture. Our religion is ancient in that it is "the faith that was once for all entrusted to the saints" (Jude 3b). It is future in that it's being played out in a spiritual atmosphere of innovation and change. The people of God are directed to be continually about the new thing that God is doing. (See Isaiah 43:19.) "Sing to him a new song" (Psalm 33:3a) is an expression echoed throughout Scripture. (See Psalms 96:1; 98:1; 144:9; 149:1; and Revelation 5:9; 14:3.)

UnLearning churches are living the mandate of winning the lost and setting the oppressed free. Like the four friends who brought the paralyzed man to Jesus (Mark 2:3), these prophetic communities bring to Jesus people who will then grow in authentic community and become empowered to serve.

Each of these faith communities articulates and practices its unique call and identity. The dominant expression of Christianity at Ginghamsburg is service. People primarily express their faith in Jesus by serving in a multitude of ways. For other churches that unique call might be a healing ministry or the sending out of daughter churches.

What is the primary expressive call and identity of your church? I want you to identify it as you read this book. But be warned: The new generation of emerging churches defies the old identities. These churches don't fit known categories. They're tough to label.

WHAT'S YOUR "ONE THING"?

Your specific mission won't necessarily be the same as mine. The shorthand version of my personal mission statement is to connect people fully with their God-destiny. It's what makes me smile. It's what gets me up in the morning. It's my one thing. It's my one best sermon.

What's yours? Try to put your finger on it as you experience this book.

I also encourage you to make specific commitments to spiritual growth. When I realized that renewal and change are based on prayer, I made a commitment to get up early each morning to pray and listen to God. I've kept that promise since August 17, 1994, following the model of Jesus in Mark 1:35: "In the morning, while it was still very dark, he got up and went out to a deserted place, and there he prayed."

UnLearning Moment

Reflect on your life mission. State the one thing you're willing to give your life and die for, as you pursue God's mission for your life.

At the conclusion of each chapter, you'll be asked to make a journal entry about what you are unLearning. The purpose of this insert is to invite you to begin wrestling with tough issues.

During the Lenten season of 2000, I did something new. I went into a forty-day season of fasting, excluding Sundays. God wanted to do a new thing in my life personally, and I knew that fasting would be crucial for me to discover it. It was a limited fast, but I am convinced that many spiritual benefits came as a result of that time of seeking God.

I'm also exploring new horizons through my leadership role at church. As I write this chapter, my immediate focus can be summarized by the words *spirit, staff,* and *space*. I'm concentrating on spiritual depth, on the staff development needed to drive the DNA of the movement out to the edges of the congregation, and on the space we are able to creatively use to accomplish the mission through the local church.

What about you? As you grow spiritually, I hope you'll be able to sharpen your own ministry focus for the next twelve months.

UNPREDICTABLE AS FIRE

In Old Testament times, fire often signified God's presence. When Moses led the Israelites through the desert, God was as close as a cloud during the day and a pillar of fire during the night. Moses explained, "You, O Lord, are in the midst of this people; for you, O Lord, are seen face to face, and your cloud stands over them and you go in front of them, in a pillar of cloud by day and in a pillar of fire by night" (Numbers 14:14b).

When the people saw the fire, they remembered God's promise of daily provision, protection, and power for living. When God moved, they moved. When God stopped, they stopped, even for months at a time. (See Numbers 9:15-23.)

The idea was to place themselves at the heart of God's leadership and direction. At that time the fire was limited to one place, usually above the tent where

they met for worship.

So was God's presence through the Holy Spirit. The Spirit came upon Moses, and sometimes others, such as the time God promised Moses, "I will take some of the spirit that is on you and put it on them" (Numbers 11:17b).

When Jesus was on planet Earth, the Holy Spirit in him was limited to one physical body. Jesus could be in only one place at a time. When he was healing people in Capernaum, he couldn't be touching people in Jerusalem.

When Jesus ascended to heaven and sent the Holy Spirit to earth in a new way, everything changed. Because of Pentecost, the Holy Spirit has been made available to all people. No longer is God merely *with* us; now God is *in* us. As Paul told the Christians in Rome about their relationship to God, "The Spirit of God dwells in you. Anyone who does not have the Spirit of Christ does not belong to him" (Romans 8:9b; see also 1 Corinthians 3:16).

Today, because we're the body of Christ, Jesus can be everywhere we are, all around the world at the same time. We are literally the body of Christ on earth, where people come and experience love, acceptance, forgiveness, freedom from fear, release from guilt and discouragement, delivery from loneliness, and empowerment for living.

The church, as the body of Christ, is led by that same Holy Spirit. We follow God's leading, much like God's people of old did in following the pillar of fire.

My CONTINUAL quest IS TO STAY FOCUSED ON THE HORIZON, watching WHERE GOD IS MOVING.

I want to see where God is taking the church next.

God intends for churches to move much less predictably than most usually do. As Jesus said, "The wind blows where it chooses...So it is with everyone who is born of the Spirit "(John 3:8). When we follow the Spirit, we become willing to innovate, re-create, reassess, step out, and risk going wherever God is.

As we unLearn, we may defy many old categories and familiar identities. Your church may become hard to label, just as a fire from heaven is hard to fit into a box.

One Church That's UnLearning

Church of the Resurrection, Leawood, Kansas

www.cor.org

QUICK DESCRIPTION: A Christian community where non-religious and nominally religious people are becoming deeply committed Christians.

HISTORY: United Methodist; started in 1990.

ATTENDANCE: 5,500-6,000 in six worship services

THEME: Hard-to-Define Worship Styles

WHAT THE LEADER SAYS: "We've unLearned the definitions of *traditional* and *contemporary* in worship. People like to choose between the two, so we advertise both. We offer nontraditional traditional worship and contemporary worship with a traditional twist. Both contain a strong focus on relevancy, sensitivity to the unchurched, and openness to the work of the Holy Spirit. In contemporary worship, we use the ancient symbols and an occasional liturgical element. In traditional worship, we avoid responsive readings or elements that seem empty or dry. In both we explain the significance of hymns, symbols, or sacraments to help new Christians and long-time Christians gain a deep appreciation for them. For neither worship style do we follow a lectionary cycle in preaching.

"The traditional services reach the largest number of unchurched people in our community. Worship—traditional or contemporary—seems dead when people don't understand it. We want people to sense the presence of the Holy Spirit, relevancy, and joy."

—Adam Hamilton, senior pastor, has been with the church since the beginning; age late thirties.

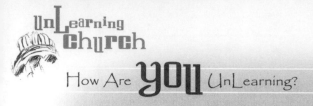

How Are **you** UnLearning?

- As you read this chapter, what are you hearing God say through the Holy Spirit? *affirmation*

- What new dreams are emerging in the eyes of your heart?
  humility

- What must you unLearn (repent or let go of) to make this happen?

- What risk will unLearning require?

ENDNOTES

1. Michael G. Maudlin, "God's Contractor," Christianity Today (14 June, 1999), www.christianitytoday.com/ct/9t7/9t7044.html
2. C. Kirk Hadaway, Penny Long Marier, and Mark Chaves, "What the Polls Don't Show: A Closer Look at U.S. Church Attendance," American Sociological Review, vol. 58, no. 6 (6 December, 1993), 741-752.
3. Reginald W. Bibby, *There's Got to Be More: Connecting Churches and Canadians* (Winfield, BC: Wood Lake Books, Inc., 1995), 16.

From Broadcast to Narrowcast

Our culture today is all about personalization. UnLearning churches focus on personalized pathways of discipleship that meet individual needs, rather than one-size-fits-all programs for the masses.

God takes ordinary things and uses them to offer powerful hope. When Jesus saw the man who was blind from birth, "he spat on the ground and made mud with the saliva and spread the mud on the man's eyes, saying to him, 'Go, wash in the pool of Siloam' " (John 9:6b 7a). The man went, washed, and came back able to see.

Jesus healed the man's eyes with mud and spit.

IN THE HANDS OF GOD, THE ordinary BECOMES extraordinary.

I'm unLearning the idea that God works only in places set apart for spiritual purposes, such as church buildings. Just as Jesus used mud and spit, today God still uses everyday people in ordinary places to do the work needed. God matches these raw resources to the need represented at any particular time and place.

You and I live at a critical juncture in time. Our culture is at a crossroads. September 11, 2001, has forever altered our modern sense of safety and security. The world is postmodern in the sense that people view the cosmos as too complex to be defined and explained by the scientific method. They also see an inherent spiritual quality about life and the world order. Oprah Winfrey's consistent theme is to "remember your spirit." Movies such as *The Sixth Sense* are overtly spiritual. The number of books dealing with "soul care" issues grows larger each year.

PEOPLE TODAY ARE INTERESTED IN spirituality BUT NOT NECESSARILY IN CHRISTIANITY.

People of today's postmodern era are experiencing an identity crisis. On the one hand, they demonstrate an intense spiritual hunger left by the vacuum of modernity. On the other hand, they are open to a cafeteria-style spirituality that consists of whatever works.

MOST ARE LOOKING outside the Christian faith

TO FIND A SENSE OF SPIRITUAL CONNECTION.

Postmoderns are seeking an experience of the "Mysterious Other" but believe the religion of the church to be restricting.

ORGANIZED RELIGION IS not WORKING.

Christianity is no longer growing in this country. The number of people in attendance weekly in United Methodist churches has been declining for years—dramatically so. The same is true in most other mainline denominations.

Even the Southern Baptists, who are the largest Protestant body in America because they've learned how to grow through any type of adversity, declined in 1998 for the first time in more than seventy years.[1]

Today's church is also aging.

WE'RE STILL SETTING our agenda

BY THE DEMOGRAPHICS

OF THE BABY BOOMERS

—those born from 1946 to 1964. In my experience, the successful growth churches of the 1980s and 1990s are usually made up of people in their forties and older. These people are primarily a modern-era audience, from which many of us are still taking our cues.

UNLEARNING FROM THOSE UNDER THIRTY-FIVE

Moderns and postmoderns will continue alongside each other for some time. But to continue to take our cues from boomers will cause us to miss the next generation.

To understand the seismic shift in today's changing worldview, we have to focus on the under-thirty-five age group. More than anyone alive today, they tend to connect with what postmodernity is all about.

Many current attempts at renewal are still repeating what they did in the 1980s and 1990s when many baby boomers were reconnecting with church.

Jesus Christ is the same YESTERDAY, TODAY, AND TOMORROW, BUT THE CULTURAL LANGUAGE IS continually changing.

The formulas of the 1980s and 1990s won't work for the future with the millennial generations.

Two years ago, I began to examine emerging churches that are relating to the next demographic group. The focus in these churches has shifted away from the effective twentieth-century models that attracted large crowds to "hear" the gospel message. These emerging churches are communities of personalization. They focus on meeting the real needs of people, offering Christ's life-transforming power.

Their most durable impact in shaping the future will be in this message to us boomers: IF YOU THINK the goal IS MERELY TO BUILD LARGE CHURCHES WITH GREAT MUSIC, INCREDIBLE DRAMAS, AND MEDIA PRESENTATIONS, YOU MAY FORGET THE REAL BUSINESS YOU'RE IN—radical life transformation THROUGH THE POWER OF GOD. IT'S ALL ABOUT SPIRIT, NOT SIZE!

UnLearning Moment

What is one boomer-era practice that you are unlearning in order to more effectively interact with the next generation?

THIRD-WAVE CHURCHES

Bob Buford, founder of Leadership Network, wrote a foreword to one of my previous books, *Real Followers*.[2] In it he calls the next generation of churches third-wave churches. They are the ones effectively reaching pre-Christian people. You've not heard of most of them yet. They're under the radar because they're under one thousand in attendance. But they represent the wave of the future.

As Buford describes it, "The first wave...was one of *replication*. The church in the United States started as an import from Europe." Immigrants from Western Europe simply relocated their traditions, dogmas, methodologies, and worship styles with them as they moved. They were literally transplanted from one continent to another.

The second wave, currently at its apex according to Buford, is *proclamation*. This was born out of the first and second Great Awakening in the United States and reached its zenith in the megachurch movement. It is based on a platform-proclaimer who gives a presentation to spectator-receivers who watch and process it. The megachurch mastered this medium through music, drama, and powerful teaching. The emphasis is on broadcast to the masses—the gathering of the crowds.

The third wave, representing the new thing God is doing, is *demonstration*.

THESE ARE CHURCHES OF
contagious faith LIVING OUT
authentic biblical community
EXPRESSED THROUGH COMPASSIONATE SERVICE AND SOCIAL JUSTICE.

"Christianity in this context is more pastoral and more hands-on," says Buford. "It's an anywhere and anytime connection."[3] The emphasis is not so much on gathering of crowds as speaking to individuals. Like the Internet, it's highly personal and interactive. Because relationship is highly personal, the emphasis is not so much on broadcast to the masses as on narrowcast to the individual.

THE HIGH LEVEL OF PERSONALIZATION COMPELS THE CHURCH TO
BECOME indigenous to its community.

IDENTIFYING THE CUSTOMER

Our culture today is increasingly one of personalization. Technology has gone from broadcast to narrowcast. Television and radio as forms of mass communication are now competing with the more personal and interactive Internet. Faith Popcorn refers to the current climate as the economy of "ego-nomics."[4]

Everything about our culture is becoming more personalized. Levi's creates special-order jeans designed to specific measurements[5], and Dell builds a computer just for your specifications. They meet individuals in the now where we live, according to our schedules, not at the convenience of the retail establishment.

E-commerce and stock trading do more than offer 24/7 service available to fit your particular schedules. Their home pages recommend a host of choices.

Many allow us to personalize the look and content of those home pages, making them even more personalized the next time we return. We even get to name them "My Fidelity," "My AOL Personal Finance" or "My CitiCorp." Web sites that focus on everything from auction shopping to hobbies encourage similar personalization. They know exactly who the customer is.

During the age of modernity, the great revivals were based on broadcast. The idea was to assemble large groups of people to hear a great presenter, from Jonathan Edwards to Dwight L. Moody, Luis Palau, T.D. Jakes, and Billy Graham. In more recent years, evangelists have used radio and television waves to broadcast their message to the masses.

The Internet is the epitome of speaking to the individual—when you want, what you want, where you want to go. One of Microsoft's huge advertising campaigns centered around the simple question, "Where do *you* want to go today?"

Business understands that it cannot focus on the masses. It has unLearned the starting point of attracting crowds and replaced it with meeting individuals at the point of their felt needs in the now.

IN THE TWENTY-FIRST-CENTURY WORLD,
YOU HAVE TO THINK smaller TO GROW bigger.

FIFTY THOUSAND PERSONALIZED "HITS" AT GINGHAMSBURG—AND GROWING

Our www.ginghamsburg.org site supports more than two dozen different on-line fellowship communities. Some are broad-based classifications. For example, several hundred people from around the globe converse weekly about the use of media and technology in the local church. They help one another sort out the details of media ministry.

Others are highly focused, like new members and hospitality ministries, and have attracted a smaller, more intimate group of regular contributors.

YOU CAN MEET REAL PEOPLE globally
IN HIGHLY PERSONALIZED WAYS,
ALL IN THE CYBER-NOW,
WHATEVER YOUR INTEREST AND STYLE.

Within two years of launching our Ginghamsburg Web site, the number of weekly users matched the number of people on premises each weekend. By the third year, it exceeded our campus attendance by more than ten times!

By each Sunday evening, the weekend's sermon is online. Here I live in an obscure town in Ohio, and we receive more than fifty thousand visits representing forty different countries to our site each month (late 2001 statistics). All these visitors can see, hear, or read the preaching.

Recently I received an e-mail from a young Japanese student, a Buddhist, writing from his dorm room in Japan. He was asking about something I had said about Jesus that he picked up in my sermon. His culture sees spirituality in a very quiet, personal way. The Internet gives him the opportunity to explore it in the context of safe space.

FAR MORE OPTIONS THAN THE INTERNET

Today's approach to narrowcasting is certainly not limited to the Internet. The new generation of emerging churches is connecting in deeply personal ways with real people in the churches' local communities.

One Sunday afternoon my wife, Carolyn, and I were taking a walk in our neighborhood. One of the houses we'd always liked was up for sale and had signs for an open house, so we went inside. "What kind of work do you do?" the realtor asked us. I told her I am the pastor at Ginghamsburg.

"I went to a divorce-recovery class there," she replied.

BY NARROWCASTING, WE HAD MET HER AT HER

point of felt need

IN THE NOW.

How specific can your narrowcasting be? Ginghamsburg even does a divorce-recovery group for kids from broken homes. We call it Kid's Hope. It's a support group for elementary children whose parents are experiencing separation or divorce. It meets weekly and is open to anyone from the church or community.

A typical evening begins as the Kid's Hope staff interacts with the parents when they are dropping off their kids. The boys and girls, after being warmly greeted, draw pictures that portray their moods. Some of the kids come in with a lot of anger and frustration about what's happening in their homes. The picture time helps the children begin to process these feelings.

The staff then offers a devotional time on a teaching theme, followed by activities in which the kids have the opportunity to develop relationships. The meeting concludes with a "group hope" prayer in which the kids themselves pray. Part of their prayer is the following sentence that they've memorized and say together as a group: "Help me to remember, Lord, that nothing is going to happen today that you and I can't handle together."

"I'd never really talked to a group of people about what I was feeling," said an elementary-aged girl in the group. "It has been nice to talk to people who can help me with what's going on with the problems in my life," said another. "Once you talk with somebody, it makes you feel better than when you keep it all inside," another child confided.

Parents feel equally helped: "It has given me a tremendous peace of mind to know that my daughter has found a place where she feels safe to talk about her feelings and where she feels connected and understood. She is more comfortable and settled in her situation, and she doesn't feel so alone because she realizes she's *not* alone."

On a different level, the unpaid staff receives help and encouragement as well. "Through the weeks, you actually see progress in their lives," said one of the leaders. "For most of these children, this is the first difficult thing they've faced in their lives, and they need to know that God will be there for them. It brings us smiles as they discover just how close God can be."

LEARNING FROM STREETWISE PEOPLE

Today's marketing gurus understand that today's culture isn't looking for information about products. Just how much could you write down about a Nike shoe after watching one of its television ads? Today's culture isn't looking to understand. Nike commercials don't talk about or even show athletic apparel. Instead, they offer a thirty-second experience.

Can we learn anything from Nike? Jesus tells us, "Learn from the shrewd manager over there." *The Message* paraphrase describes the shrewd managers as "streetwise people...on constant alert, looking for angles." (See Luke 16:1-9.) Are we still broadcasting information about religion when people really want an invitation to an experience of God? We must offer a personalized pathway of discipleship that is designed to meet people's individual needs.

One Church That's
UnLearning

Axxess, part of Pantego Bible Church, Fort Worth, Texas
www.axxess.org, www.pantego.org

QUICK DESCRIPTION: A new approach to ministry that will engage the current postmodern culture.

HISTORY: nondenominational; Pantego Bible Church began in 1906; Axxess began in 1996.

ATTENDANCE: two hundred in one service on Sunday evening

THEME: Personalizing the Gospel

WHAT THE LEADER SAYS: "We've unLearned the way we do evangelism. The Gospel story must live in our lives; it dies when it is broadcast or passed without human contact. The idea of objective, absolute truth is dead for those we are trying to reach. Truth cannot be disembodied anymore; it must be incarnated for people to embrace it. The last hundred years in the United States have been a period of tremendous *proclamation* of the Gospel, but the next hundred years will most likely be marked as a period of tremendous *demonstration* of it.

"We don't operate by mission; we have built around relationships—and by the gifts we see in our people. We try to measure by the quality of our relationships; we don't measure effectiveness in typical ways. We have chosen to focus on a Central Person (the person of Christ) rather than on a central theology."

—*Brad Cecil, Axxess Pastor since 1996, on "mother church" staff since 1991; age late thirties.*

How Are *you* UnLearning?

• As you transition from modern "broadcasting" to postmodern "narrowcasting," identify one attitude you are helping your congregation unLearn.

• What new values are they replacing it with?

• Which thought or sentence in this chapter strikes you most keenly?

ENDNOTES

1. Linda Lawson, "Southern Baptist church membership declines for the first time since 1926" (www.bpnews.net/bpnews.asp?ID=1161)
2. Mike Slaughter with Warren Bird, *Real Followers* (Nashville, TN: Abingdon Press, 1999), 15.
3. Slaughter, *Real Followers*, 16.
4. Faith Popcorn and Lys Marigold, *Clicking* (New York, NY: HarperCollins Publishers, 1996). 145.
5. www.levi.com/original_spin

Thriving in Paradox

The church of the last five hundred years has lived in an "either-or" world called modernity. The postmodern church embraces the "both-and" of paradox, where two seemingly contradictory attitudes exist at the same time.

Jesus taught that his life mission would take him to a cruel and painful death and then he would rise from the dead. His first followers recognized the importance of his coming back to life. "If Christ has not been raised, then our proclamation has been in vain and your faith has been in vain," said the Apostle Paul (1 Corinthians 15:14).

The paradox of the "living dead" is still with us today. Jesus' followers must experience the presence of the one who came out of the tomb. We are to consider ourselves "dead to sin and alive to God in Christ Jesus" (Romans 6:11). "But if Christ is in you, though the body is dead because of sin, the Spirit is life because of righteousness" (Romans 8:10).

Jesus' death and resurrection created a huge paradox, where two seemingly contradictory things exist at the same time. Remember, empty tombs don't make sense. We can't prove the Resurrection rationally.

The church of the last five hundred years has lived in an "either-or" world called modernity, ever since the invention of the printing press and the dawning of the Enlightenment.

THE MODERN CHURCH HAS TRIED TO MASTER the art of explanation.

Its love affair with tight logic and ordered reasons for faith has seriously downplayed the paradoxes in Jesus' teaching and in the church he created. Can logic ever really explain how our Savior can be completely God and completely human at the same time? We have much unLearning to do.

The modern understanding of the universe reigned until the 1970s and 1980s, when people's worldviews began to enter a time of revolutionary change. We no longer call today's period the modern era but the postmodern era—a time of people who are far more eager to live in paradox and mystery.

It doesn't make sense to live out of only the cerebral part of our beings. God created us with far more complexity. We are people of mystery who live in a creation of mystery and serve a God of mystery.

The postmodern church, like the early church, lives in the "both-and" of paradox.

THE EMERGING CHURCH CELEBRATES mystery MORE THAN EXPLANATION.

Here are some of the "both-ands" that the emerging church is unLearning.

BOTH ANCIENT AND FUTURE

For the leaders of tomorrow's church, this world of paradox represents an ancient-future church. It's stained glass *and* media screen. It's candles *and* stage lights together. It's secular *and* sacred. Former pastor and futurologist Bill Easum predicts that "worship will become more Eastern and more high tech...The issue is no longer is it contemporary or is it traditional. Now, does it have spirit? Does it have the mystery of the east and the high-tech of the west? Can it say it all with words? If so, it has missed the point."[1]

BOTH HIGH TECH AND HIGH TOUCH

Tomorrow's churches are *both* high tech *and* high touch. Like the Internet, the faith communities of emerging churches are highly interactive and deeply personal.

Through technology,

CHURCHES THAT ARE PART OF THE POSTMODERN AGE

CAN ALSO invite the outside world

TO BE INVOLVED IN THEIR QUEST FOR GOD.

Many times each year, Ginghamsburg sends a camera team to a nearby town—Dayton, Columbus, or Cincinnati. We ask such questions as "What is hard about faith?" and "Why do you—or don't you—go to church?" Then we edit the responses into a short video that we use as part of our worship celebrations, designed around a particular theme.[2]

Sometimes we recognize friends or co-workers in these "on the street" video shots. We use this medium not to draw attention to technology but because it

provides cultural relevance. As Kim Miller, Ginghamsburg's creative director, explains:

> *Gone are the days when even church folks could listen to one or two people (better known as talking heads). Now, using technology, the world can become our "cast"... Suddenly we're not just imagining what we think people are feeling on a subject, but we have the real deal to watch and listen to. Participation goes to a whole new level. High-tech serves high-touch.*[3]

We make certain that the people-stories we tell via video lift up the core values and DNA of Ginghamsburg Church, such as the value of serving. When one of our home groups became involved with a group of young teenage men in a foster home, we asked someone to tell the story of what they were doing. We created a video of the story and played it as a "Mission Moment" prior to receiving the offerings. We feature such things then because people are more inclined to give toward an organization or ministry that is involved in genuine life change. Money follows mission, not budget.

As the video story unfolds, we see one of the church's home groups, eager to reach out beyond itself, invite eight at-risk youths to come to church with them. They bring these young men to Ginghamsburg for worship celebration and to The Avenue (our youth activities center) to play basketball. The video lets us experience the electricity of the connection—the guys don't want to go home!

The home group loves it too. "We did it as a one-time event, but it kept going," says one person from the home group. "I walked away so blessed after spending one afternoon with them." So they take it a step further and offer to go to the young men's foster home to eat cookies and study the Bible together. The group experienced the joy of building trust through relationships, of speaking to the young men about Christ, and of leading them in a direction they weren't going before. "My relationship with Christ has completely changed because of my experiences and times with these boys," says one of the women in the group. "They feel like family to us."

Then we hear the account of one of the young men coming to faith in Christ. He concludes, "I never really cared about what happened in life, but now that I have a relationship with God, it's much easier to get along and not become mad so easily."

High-tech, high-touch combinations like this happen all over. Emerging churches are not afraid to use technology, but they understand that technology is for the purpose of telling stories that connect people to an experience of God, authentic community, and life purpose.

Ginghamsburg embraces technology and excellence, but never for the purpose of presentation alone. We use the storytelling abilities of technology, along with a passion for excellence, for the purpose of more effectively connecting people with an experience of God. It maximizes participation.

When The Wall Street Journal wanted to study how technology has changed the way people attend church, it profiled Ginghamsburg. A reporter interviewed people about their experience of worship celebration at Ginghamsburg. She noted that high-tech worship celebration is more than saying, "Let us pray, watch movies, and listen to a killer band." We experience highly personalized media pieces connected with prayer, music, and interaction. She noted that additional high-touch occurs at Ginghamsburg through more than two hundred adult cell groups and through online personalized fellowship communities on our Web site.[4]

We are not alone in making this transition. Consider the evolution Kim Miller observed between Johnny Carson and Jay Leno. On the earlier The Tonight Show, the talent was limited to Johnny Carson, Ed McMahon, the current guest, and occasionally the bandleader. The 2001 version of The Tonight Show with Jay Leno lets the entire audience become the cast, along with the camera people, directors, band, and local store owners in the community.[5] (The Late Show with David Letterman does the same thing.) They are accomplishing a high-touch experience with extremely high-tech tools.

UnLearning Moment

Think of one high-tech element your church has embraced. How can it become a high-touch tool?

BOTH LEADER AND TEAMS

The structure of postmodern churches includes *both* strong spiritual leaders *and* ministry experienced through empowered teams. Most churches of the 1950s, 1960s, and 1970s were board-led. Many of the effective models of the 1980s and 1990s viewed the pastor as the chief executive officer who told everyone else, "It's my way, or the highway to find your way to another church!"

I've repented of that attitude because Christians were never called to adapt the church to business-organizational models. Spiritual leadership is radically different from the notion of pastor-as-CEO.

Today's paradox involves a strong spiritual leader who provides clarity of vision and tenacity of purpose while at the same time attracting a competent, creative team of people who dream, develop, and deploy the mission in tandem with the leader.

BOTH LOCAL AND GLOBAL

Postmodern churches are *both* local *and* global. People might be more connected to the church where they log on, not where they attend. If George Barna's research projections hold true, more than 100 million people will soon be looking to the Internet for spiritual nourishment.[6]

We know of many people who live in other parts of the world who may be affiliated with another church, but the primary source of their God experience is Ginghamsburg. One lady in Australia e-mailed us, asking us if we could tweak the layout of the printed version so it would come out more cleanly for her. She explained, "I download them and print them from 'my church' "—referring to Ginghamsburg—"to give them to the people in my neighborhood"—referring to her friends eleven thousand miles from Ohio!

Mike Gibbs, a former member of Ginghamsburg, moved to Florida several years ago and is active in a church there. However, he's continued as an unofficial leader of our Internet-based fellowship online community, designed for people who want to chat about Ginghamsburg's weekly message—which is available in both video streaming and text formats. Like them, he experiences the sermons on the Internet. When people ask for help understanding our worship celebrations or my sermons, Mike Gibbs explains them better than I could. Yet he doesn't attend Ginghamsburg in person!

BOTH CONSERVATIVE AND LIBERAL

Postmodern churches are politically *both* conservative *and* liberal. I've been at Ginghamsburg more than twenty-two years, and even long-timers don't know whether I vote Republican or Democrat. I like to irritate both sides!

I've often felt like I don't have a home in the institutional church. Churches tend to build themselves around ideas and causes, such as political parties.

In Jesus' day, THE PHARISEES BELIEVED EVERYTHING AND MORE, WHILE THE SADDUCEES BELIEVED NOTHING AND LESS.

Jesus was neither. The emerging leader is neither.

UnLearning churches seat conservatives and liberals next to each other.

At a recent conference sponsored by Ginghamsburg, participants came from some thirty different denominational groups and ten different countries. A hundred years ago, our focus would have been on our differences, and we would not have met together. Today members of a theologically conservative church denomination might not even know or care that they are worshipping and learning alongside representatives from denominations on the other side of the spectrum. Instead their main interest is what has brought them together: the commonality of our faith and commitment to Jesus Christ.

BOTH CATHOLIC AND EVANGELICAL

Postmodern churches are *both* Catholic *and* evangelical. We did a quick survey one weekend and found that more than nine hundred people who attend Ginghamsburg (a United Methodist church) view their primary religious identity as Roman Catholic! Many go to Mass as well as participate with us in the same weekend.

We had two liturgical Ash Wednesday worship celebrations in March of 2001, and the room was packed both times. It was the biggest response to date. People came from all over the community. Many already had ashes on their foreheads, indicating that they had been to Mass at a Catholic church already that morning. Their number included Tom Lipps, our assistant music director, who remains an active Catholic.

We teach that a person comes into relationship with God through faith. "As it is written, 'The one who is righteous will live by faith' " (Romans 1:17b). We emphasize, as did John Wesley, the gift of grace: "For by grace you have been saved through faith, and this is not your own doing; it is the gift of God—not the result of works" (Ephesians 2:8-9a). And we welcome people from all faith backgrounds to come alongside us in Christ, whether their heritage is Protestant, Catholic, Orthodox, or other.

"For centuries, the one sure way to tell a Catholic from a Protestant was to look for the dark smudge on the forehead on Ash Wednesday," began a recent Boston Globe article on changes in religious observances. "No more. Reflecting an increasing demand for ritual and decreasing hostility toward Catholicism among Protestants, a growing number of Protestant churches today will be offering worshipers the traditional sign of penitence and mourning."

" 'Five-hundred years ago we gave up these rituals because we didn't want to

be Catholic, and now we're saying there was a loss for us spiritually,' said Susan P. Dickerman of the Massachusetts Conference of the United Church of Christ. 'There's a tremendous yearning for developing spirituality.' "[7]

BOTH CONTEMPORARY AND CROSS-GENERATIONAL

Postmodern churches are *both* contemporary *and* cross-generational. The big thing of the 1990s was to have baby boomer churches, Generation X churches, and gatherings specifically targeted to other age splits. Postmodern churches are cross-generational. They celebrate the paradox of the differences between generations.

When Ginghamsburg first launched a Saturday-night worship celebration, like many others, we predicted that it would draw a crowd of singles and young families. We were wrong. There are more senior adults than young people on Saturday nights. One Saturday night, after we had just played "Higher" by the secular rock group Creed ("Can you take me higher, to the place where blind men see? Can you take me higher, to the place with golden streets?"), I couldn't resist asking a seventy-five-year-old man why he was there.

"What do you mean?" he asked.

"Well, the music is loud and really contemporary," I replied.

"What kind of music do you think I listen to?" he asked in reply. I knew he didn't come from a churched background, so I didn't even try to guess.

"When I was twenty, Elvis arrived, and when I was thirty, the Beatles hit the scene, and I liked them," he replied. "I've been raised on contemporary music, and that's what you have here," he concluded.

I thought of my growing-up years at home. Our staples were Herb Alpert and the Tijuana Brass and Diana Ross. Suddenly I realized that seventy-five-year-olds, except the minority who were raised in the church, have known nothing but contemporary culture.[8] Who have we in the church been listening to: the musical preferences of the choir, or those God tells us to go out and find?

UnLearning churches are cross-generational rather than separate and distinct. One summer we invited the community to a get-acquainted event on our church campus. Our Welcome Tent featured a swing band. To our surprise, people in their seventies were dancing alongside teenagers. We sent one of our camera teams out to get people's responses to the day. One older woman summarized the significance of what we were trying to do: "It's encouraging to know that even at my age I'm not done yet. I've been in lots of churches in my life. I've encountered more changed lives here because Ginghamsburg opens its arms and doors to all kinds of people who want to find out what's going on with Jesus."

BOTH SINNERS AND SAINTS

Postmodern churches are for *both* sinners *and* saints together. Duplicating the most popular church-growth models of the 1980s and 1990s, many churches offered separate services for seekers and believers. Today's churches are becoming both believer-focused and seeker-focused at the same time. It's good and bad together, just like the kingdom of God, where Jesus says to go into the streets and invite *everyone* to God's party: " 'The wedding is ready, but those invited were not worthy. Go therefore into the main streets, and invite everyone you find to the wedding banquet.' Those slaves went out into the streets and gathered all whom they found, *both good and bad*; so the wedding hall was filled with guests" (Matthew 22:8b-10, emphasis added). This parable affirms the paradox of God-experiences for believers and seekers at the same time.

The people who had the hardest time catching on were the Pharisees. Jesus condemned the religious leaders for locking people out of the "party" when they weren't even experiencing the party themselves! "When others are going in, you stop them," Jesus said (Matthew 23:13b).

God's word to us today is, "Don't shut the door to the party!" Or as Jesus explained elsewhere, the good wheat and the bad weeds will grow together until God separates them later at harvest time. (See Matthew 13:24-28.)

INCARNATION IS THE PLACE

where sacred and secular meet.

Some people accuse next-generation churches of dumbing down the Gospel. Isn't that God's intent? When the infinite God becomes finite and puts it on a level where I can get it, the proper term to use is "dumbing down."

God DUMBED IT DOWN

WITHOUT WATERING IT DOWN.

The Gospel is offensive, but we need to put it in a language so that people recognize that they've been offended!

Jesus came to earth because God loved us with reckless abandonment. It's a love beyond self-preservation. "For God so loved the world that he gave his only Son, so that everyone who believes in him may not perish but may have eternal life" (John 3:16).

The incarnation means that God became a man in the person of Jesus. You could even say that God was obsessed with love and passion over losing us. How obsessed? God became a human being, came after us, and was even willing to die on a cross. God showed us a go-for-broke, willing-to-be-hung-out-there, with-everything-you've-got kind of passion, without regard for life or limb. That's God's love for you and me.

The idea of a God who would offer love like that is beyond reason. God's love draws us into a world of paradox.

One Church That's
UnLearning

Graceland at Santa Cruz Bible Church, Santa Cruz, California
www.santacruzbible.org and www.vintagefaith.com

QUICK DESCRIPTION: A ministry of Santa Cruz Bible Church specifically designed to bring the ancient truths of the Christian faith to emerging generations in a postmodern world.

HISTORY: nondenominational; Santa Cruz Bible started in 1884; Graceland started in 1997.

ATTENDANCE: eight hundred in two Sunday-evening services

THEME: Vintage Christianity

WHAT THE LEADER SAYS: "One important value we've had to unLearn is the aesthetics of worship to reach postmoderns. In a seeker-sensitive model, which God tremendously used in the 80s and 90s, the idea is to create a worship environment that doesn't look or feel like 'church.' Therefore churches removed religious symbols, added theater seats, and designed new worship centers with modern architecture and comfort.

"However, these are the very things we need to reach the emerging culture, who are looking for a spiritual experience and something ancient. We brought back stained-glass images on video screens. When people enter, darkness and candles communicate that something spiritual will happen here. We built crosses as ancient symbols of faith. We also lowered the stage where the band and preaching takes place to be closer to where the people sit.

"We unLearned the message as the centerpiece of a worship service, even though it is still forty minutes of the 1³/₄ hour service. Because the experiential is so important, we design the worship service to be more organic than linear. The message is but one part of the total 'experience.' We incorporate as many interactive elements as possible, so people don't come just to sit and listen passively. We had to learn that it is OK to have periods of silence. We allow people to get on their knees if they want to pray. Worship isn't so much of a smooth-running program as an experiential, participatory response."

—*Dan Kimball, Lead pastor since beginning of Graceland, on staff with Santa Cruz Bible Church since 1989; age early forties.*

How Are you UnLearning?

- How are you currently experiencing paradox in your own context? How can you celebrate your paradox?

- How are you unLearning so that you can provide clarity of vision and tenacity of purpose for your church?

ENDNOTES

1. *Emerging Trends for Effective Ministry in the 21st Century Church*, American Society for Church Growth, 11/2000, side one.
2. A collection of video clips from Ginghamsburg titled *The Visual Edge* is available through Group Publishing. For this video and other printed and video resources, go to www.ginghamsburg.org
3. Mike Slaughter and Kim Miller, "Next Level Churches—a Multisensory Experience," Rev (Sept-Oct, 2000), 84.
4. Patricia Davis, "How Technology Has Changed the Way We Attend Church," The Wall Street Journal (13 November, 2000), R28-R29.
5. Slaughter, "Next Level Churches—a Multisensory Experience," 84.
6. George Barna, "More Americans Are Seeking Net-Based Faith Experiences," Barna Research Online (www.barna.org/)
7. Michael Paulson, "On Ash Wednesday, a Wider Observance," Boston Globe (28 February, 2001), www.boston.com/dailyglobe2/059/metro/on_ash_Wednesday_a_wider_observance+.shtml.
8. Ron Crandall, *The Contagious Witness: Exploring Christian Conversion* (Nashville, TN: Abingdon Press, 1999), 107-134.

Toward a Radical Christianity

UnLearning churches are based on shared life in Jesus, more than issue-centered ideology. Just like the Apostle Paul, they know nothing but Jesus crucified.

Jesus had an ancient-future perspective. He was able to look backward and forward at the same time.

In the ancient world, the people of God often used memorial stones. When God did something unforgettable, they would erect stones at the location as a point of reference. These markers reminded them of God's unfailing love and of their responsibility to God's purpose in their future journeys. The practice reminds people where they've come from, whose they are, and where they're going. Scripture warns us against moving an ancient boundary stone set up by our ancestors: "Do not move the ancient boundary marks" (Proverbs 22:28a, TLB). Markers are important.

PROBLEMS WITH ORGANIZED RELIGION

People today, both inside and outside the church, have an apathetic attitude toward organized religion. Most will tell you that it's not working.

Perhaps their lack of interest is because we institutional church people have been more skilled at building walls than at rediscovering ancient paths.

MANY OF US HAVE A POCKET FULL OF ROCKS THAT AREN'T ancient markers AT ALL.

They are just a bunch of deadweight pebbles that institutionally correct people have trained us to put into our pockets.

Are we erecting walls or identifying ancient markers? Walls confine and restrict. They keep people out.

Markers are not meant to exclude. They outline the moral-spiritual path for a twenty-first century culture at a crossroads.

Our society is marked by increased spiritual hunger and activity, yet overall attendance in churches has decreased. The lack of spiritual power in churches today makes me skeptical as well. As I look around many churches, the situation seems like the movie *Night of the Living Dead*.

MANY CHURCHES HAVE DIED,

AND SOMEONE JUST NEEDS TO TELL THEM

they're dead.

The ones still alive are asking, like the prophet Elijah, "Am I the only one left? Is there anyone out there who is being faithful to the purpose of God on planet Earth?" (See 1 Kings 19:1-10.)

Remember the guy who burst into a Baptist church in Texas? If angry people with guns are going to storm into church gatherings and shoot folks for their faith relationship with Jesus Christ, then I want to get shot for being a part of the right thing. I don't want the church I serve to sacrifice lives to something that is not world-changing. The postmodern church must erect markers, not walls, so that we can help others find the way.

What is the hope for a world at the crossroads? The Jesus perspective—an eye to the ancient and to the future at the same time.

BARE ESSENTIALS

Radical Christianity is based on two ancient boundary stones. The two biblical markers for an ancient-future church appear in 1 John 4. One is the absolute necessity to live through God's Son, Jesus. The other is to love one another.

The first marker is to experience the One who is truth. "God's love was revealed among us in this way: God sent his only Son into the world so that we might live through him" (1 John 4:9). The purpose is that we might *live* through him, not that we might merely *believe* through him.

As a child in Sunday school, I received information about the man named Jesus. My teacher gave me a little picture of Jesus. It was about the size of a baseball card. I was supposed to carry this picture in my wallet. You've probably seen the picture, found in many Protestant church buildings in the 1950s and 1960s.

I came to think about Jesus as a player featured on the baseball cards I collected. (Unfortunately, it wasn't worth as much as a baseball card!) I often wonder what would have happened if I had said to my baseball-card-collecting buddies, "I have a '58 Jesus in mint condition, what will you give me for it?"

It seemed that faith was measured by the ability to quote facts and develop knowledge about a historical player. It was just like memorizing the statistics about a baseball legend, based on information on the back of the card.

For the ancient people of God, the focus wasn't information they gained in a classroom. The ancients talked about a revolutionary encounter—"what we have heard...seen with our eyes...and touched with our hands...the eternal life that was with the Father and was revealed to us" (1 John 1:1b-2). Others made the same emphasis, such as when the Apostle Paul said, in effect, "What's happened to me isn't something I learned about in a book or learned through human teaching. Instead, God was pleased to reveal Jesus to me." (See Galatians 1:11-16.)

The test for knowing God is not whether your church articulates a correct doctrinal perspective. Nor is it whether you cuss, smoke, chew, or hang out with people who do.

THE FIRST STONE FOR THE POSTMODERN CHURCH IS new life in Christ.

"Whoever has the Son has life; whoever does not have the Son of God does not have life" (1 John 5:12). The Son of God came not so that we could believe in him but so we could live through him. For these people, Jesus was not a person sitting in some classroom where they went to learn statistical information about his life. Jesus was eternal life that had appeared in a revolutionary encounter!

The second stone is the practice of loving one another from the heart. Jesus didn't say to live in his *religion*. He said to live in his *love*!

You and I are to be the embodiment of God's love. The apostles teach us to "love one another, because love is from God; everyone who loves is born of God and knows God...Since God loved us so much, we also ought to love one another. No one has ever seen God; if we love one another, God lives in us, and his love is perfected in us" (1 John 4:7, 11-12).

How did Jesus say people would know who his disciples were? By how many times a month they serve or receive communion? By the wearing of clergy robes and vestments? By seminary degrees? By bumper stickers or offices adorned with Jesus plaques? No. By the way we love one another.

We become a demonstration of God's presence in the world.

IT'S THROUGH THE DEMONSTRATION OF God's love THAT PEOPLE WILL BE ABLE TO SEE THE INVISIBLE.

A religion editor from a local newspaper came to interview me about a conference we were having at Ginghamsburg. At the end of the interview, I asked if she went to church. I assumed she did, since she was a religion editor. She said, "No, I am a Buddhist. I was raised in the church, but about ten years ago, I became involved in Buddhism because the highest value of Buddhism is the value of compassion."

Her next comment made me feel as if she had put her hand in my chest and squeezed my heart. "The people I grew up around in the church were some of the least compassionate people I ever knew," she added. Ouch.

Yet Jesus is compassion made visible.

JESUS IS THE
highest demonstration
OF COMPASSION POSSIBLE.

If what I am connected to is not about compassion, grace, and hope, then it is not truth. The One who is Truth is unconditional love, compassion, mercy, and hope.

We who have encountered the resurrected Christ can demonstrate unconditional love because we have experienced it. Not because we've gotten so good at loving God. We're terrible at loving God! If we're honest we acknowledge that "we love because he first loved us" (1 John 4:19).

MY EXPERIENCE AT THE MARKERS

At age seventeen I couldn't see the future. All I could focus on was the draft for the Vietnam War. I used to go across the street and play pool with a guy in my neighborhood who was in his fifties and who had studied for the priesthood. There was something different—a peace—about this guy. He knew Jesus in a way I didn't.

I'D TALK ABOUT MY fears,
AND HE'D TALK ABOUT Jesus.

Sometimes you have a better chance of seeing Jesus while shooting pool than you do in the church. I said to this would-be priest, "I am going to be eighteen on my next birthday. I can't see past eighteen, and it really scares me. I think this may be some kind of premonition that I am going to die or something."

My comments opened the door for several conversations about my friend's experience with Jesus. I can't explain what happened because it wasn't like a crisis

moment, but somehow during those "close encounters," I began to experience the mystery of the powerful Jesus. My eyes were opened, and I could see the future. My heart began to beat in rhythm with God's heart.

Many people come to Jesus and then expect Jesus to become converted to *their* worldview!

GOD IS NOT THE ONE WHO NEEDS TO CHANGE.

TO EXPERIENCE JESUS IS TO TAKE ON

Jesus' worldview.

It's the mystery of the powerful Jesus.

The world is looking for an experience of God. At the same time, they are turned off by certain arrogant and harsh attitudes in the church. None of us can stand the kind of people who walk around like they have a grasp on truth, rather than acting as if the One who is Truth has grasped them.

I DO NOT POSSESS GOD,

BUT God's truth POSSESSES ME.

DIVINE LIFE HAS INVADED MY BODY.

And so eternal life divinely invaded my body, and my heart began to beat in rhythm with God's heart. It was strange. My eyes began to see through God's eyes. My mind began to think with God's mind.

I was seventeen, but I could see my future! I could see how my life was going to be used for God's purpose to touch other people. I could see God's future and plan. It wasn't like I fully understood it, but I trusted the One who did.

Today a lot of people talk about having Jesus, but Jesus must have you. Once possessed, you acquire Jesus' worldview. You take on Jesus' outlook, Jesus' perspective, and Jesus' priorities. Otherwise your Jesus becomes a Republican, a Democrat, or some other political operative.

During my first two years in college, I studied retail management. I was going to make some serious money. The next thing I knew, I found myself in the School of Social Work, working with Appalachian folks. What happened to me? Jesus transformed me. Two lives were becoming one life. It was no longer I who lived but Christ who lived in me.

That's the Jesus-transformation marker. I keep that stone in my pocket. It is an ancient truth for a world at a crossroads.

The opening words of 1 John refer to Jesus as the word of life, the Word of God.

A lot of people believe—and here is what's wrong with institutional religion—that God "spoke" (past tense) only through Scripture. True, Scripture is the Word of God, but God is still speaking (present tense) through Jesus. The prophets in the Bible never limited God to "God said long ago." They used the phrase "Thus saith the Lord." They reminded us that God is continually speaking.

THE LIVING Word of God IS IN ME,
SPEAKING RIGHT NOW.

Jesus continues to speak and to transform you and me. That is the mystery of the powerful Jesus.

UnLearning Moment

Reflect on how God is leading you today. State the one thing God is asking you to unLearn or let go of to move forward.

MARKERS FOR THE EMERGING CHURCH

Some of us have erected walls that need to come down. Others have tripped over plain old rocks that are not ancient markers but are institutional distractions, complicated methodologies, and irrelevant formulas.

We don't need more walls. We don't need more rocks to trip over that aren't real ancient markers. You and I need to be reminded that Jesus and the embodiment of love are all we really need.

IF WE'RE GOING TO BE THE CHURCH AT ALL,

LET'S BE the real thing.

Life in the emerging church is based on shared life in Jesus, not ideology. I want my tombstone to read, "Only Jesus." It's not always easy to keep our emphasis on Jesus. The church at Corinth lost that focus. They had a tendency to become sidetracked by secondary issues such as worship style and gifts of the Spirit, especially the gift of tongues.

The Apostle Paul knew that spiritual leaders keep the main thing the main thing—our life together based on Christ. So he determined when he went to the church in Corinth "to know nothing among you except Jesus Christ, and him crucified" (1 Corinthians 2:2).

Postmodern churches are not erecting walls built of layer after layer of impersonal dogmas and ideologies. The postmodern church focuses on two ancient markers: the mystery of the powerful Jesus, and the mission of love.

One Church That's UnLearning

Cedar Ridge Community Church, Spencerville, Maryland (outside Washington, D.C.)
www.crcc.org

QUICK DESCRIPTION: Cedar Ridge Community Church is a dynamic hub of Christian thought, action, community, and creative arts, dedicated to embracing and transforming our postmodern world with the message and love of Jesus Christ.

HISTORY: nondenominational; started in 1982, restarted in 1988.

ATTENDANCE: nine hundred in two Sunday-morning services

THEME: Different Worldviews on the Living Word

WHAT THE LEADER SAYS: "One of the hardest things was unLearning my assumptions about the Bible. I tried to assert the authority of Scripture to unchurched, post-Enlightenment people who had unconsciously but very strongly rejected the whole Enlightenment approach to authority. But their approach to knowledge, truth, belief, and doubt was so radically different from mine that I couldn't prove points by proof-texting or waving the Bible and saying, 'The Bible says...'

"I didn't bargain for that kind of radical rethinking when I began ministering to unchurched people. I thought we just needed to get some drums.

"Instead I've had to re-examine everything associated with doing church. My dream is to change the way people in the Washington-Baltimore region (and beyond) think about the Bible, the church, and Christianity."

—*Brian McLaren, pastor, has been with the church since its beginning; age mid-forties.*

How Are **you** UnLearning?

- Draw an image or picture of what radical Christianity looks like in your situation.

- As you interact with this chapter, what do you feel most strongly about?

- Something's gotta go! What one thing are you giving up in order to live a more radical faith?

Engaging the Senses

5

Being created in God's image makes us multisensory beings. People learn best when all their senses are engaged.
The next generation of churches will avoid the stiff and
cerebral and will offer people a multisensory experience
of God.

Jesus says that it's good for us to recognize our spiritual neediness.

NEVER IS GOD CLOSER
THAN WHEN WE ARE ACUTELY AWARE OF OUR
spiritual need.

UnLearning churches realize that people are engaged through environment and experience, enabling the maximum exchange between their need and God's fullness.

In the Sermon on the Mount as paraphrased by *The Message*, Jesus says:
"You're blessed when you're at the end of your rope. With less of you there is more
of God and his rule...You're blessed when you've worked up a good appetite for
God. He's food and drink in the best meal you'll ever eat" (Matthew 5:3, 6).

Those word pictures are a powerful translation of phrases you may have
heard before as "poor in spirit" (Matthew 5:3) and "hunger and thirst for righteousness" (Matthew 5:6). The metaphors indicate people who are aware of their
needs. They are hungry for God. They're not satisfied. They have not attained the
place they need to be. They have an incredible hunger and thirst for God.

I GO TO CHURCH BECAUSE
I need God.

My greatest hunger, the greatest need in my life, is not to be busy; it is to be
filled with the presence of God. If people don't recognize the spiritual emptiness
in their lives, staying home and sleeping might do more good. God doesn't give

frequent-pew-sitter points for coming to church. God can't design something new if it is still filled with the old.

God wants us to start empty. We've got to lead our churches to turn to God's love first. This letter reflects that discovery:

Dear Michael:

I felt I needed to send you this letter so that I may express to you and your staff my thankfulness and how very grateful my boys and I are that we have become part of the Ginghamsburg Church family. We have been attending Ginghamsburg since Easter Sunday.

I am in recovery for alcoholism, and as with many single mothers out there, the road has not been an easy one. I have been blessed by the grace of God with the gift of recovery and, as the result of a spiritual process, have been filled with God's presence.

The subject you spoke of after Easter really hit home to me because, as you, I have had the presence of God fill my life. I was hung over one morning and very sick. But this time I had vowed that I would stop drinking. My skin turned yellow, and something was really wrong with me. I did not seem to mind that my life and my children's lives had become a living hell. I was on my knees over the toilet and decided that I could not live the way I was living anymore.

I WAS READY TO TAKE MY OWN LIFE

WHEN A CALMNESS, A *peacefulness*, CAME OVER ME.

I did not know it then, but I do know it now, that it was God scooping me up into his loving and forgiving arms.

God took those pills away from me and told me that he was always with me and loved me and forgave me. My reaction was very much like yours when you were getting the bad grades in high school. "Me? You love and forgive me?"

I really thought this spirit had wandered into the wrong bathroom, for I was not worthy of love and forgiveness.

I fell down on the floor and wept as you said Paul did, for the spirit and power that was with me was stronger than anything I ever felt in my life. I was afraid that if I should move or get up, the peace and calmness would leave me, and I would be all alone again.

I slept for a while on that floor, and when I awoke the peace and calmness was still with me. It has been with me for two years now. I'm not saying that

I do not have good days and bad days, but I will tell you that with God by my side, I have no fear.

I hope you do not mind me sharing this with you. I needed to tell you "Thank you" for being my God-connector and being so honest about your meetings with God.

This woman turned first to God's love. She was empty and open. God engaged her senses, and she experienced the truth that her Creator treats her as lovable.

I need the same kind of engagement. One of the ways I hide from God is by getting into performance orientation to make up for all my years of shame. I want to say, "God, you've done a lot for me, so I'll spend my life trying to make it up to you."

God's word to me is, "Mike, just take your hands off the controls, keep turning to me and realizing your emptiness. I will create, I will design, and I will fill."

God can't fill any of us if we're filled with something else. If we can't deal with our shame, we load our hours with busyness, unfocused activity, or selfish ambition. Sometimes we focus on fixing someone else's life. All these substitutes keep us from creating an environment that's open toward God.

God's extravagant love is beyond logic. It engages our emotions.

WE'LL NEVER EXPERIENCE
the presence of God
IF WE WAIT FOR OUR MINDS TO UNDERSTAND IT.

The postmodern church opens itself to the idea that God created us as multi-sensory beings. This movement avoids the stiff and cerebral. It leads people into an experience of God that engages all their senses.

UnLearning Moment

Describe one way you could reshape your worship celebrations to invite discoveries that are similar to what the letter above described.

THE NEW AMERICAN HANGOUT

A while back I visited a Barnes & Noble bookstore in Cincinnati for the first time. I immediately smelled coffee, walked that direction, and was surprised that they were offering it for free. (When was the last time you smelled coffee in a library?) Before I accepted a cup, I saw that they had a great coffee bar. So I passed by the free stuff and bought a white chocolate cappuccino.

Then I noticed a guy playing jazz on the piano. Barnes & Noble was featuring his CDs, so I bought one.

In fact, the store carried a large music section. It was better than the CD store in my community. It included a huge bank of listening stations. And I had entered the place thinking it was a store for books only!

I went in thinking I was on a short errand to buy a magazine about log homes. I ended up hanging out in this bookstore for a couple of hours—and I came home with a shopping bag full of literature, CDs, and books.

Stores like Barnes & Noble have become more than places to spend money; they are environments where people spend the day.

the new American hangout. BOOKSTORES HAVE BECOME

In the local Barnes & Noble store, people do far more there than buy books. They stand around and meet friends. They sit in comfortable leather chairs, drink coffee, and read books while listening to live music.

Bookstores like this are more like homes or restaurants. At home you can drink coffee while reading or talking with friends.

Libraries, by contrast, are more like churches. All the libraries I've visited seemed to specialize in hard chairs, reminding me of hard-backed pews. How many churches, like libraries, think more functionally than environmentally?

I much prefer Barnes & Noble to my local library. A pastor friend, Daryl Ward, told me, "I love being surrounded by books, but libraries are too sanitary." He's right. Libraries I've visited are too quiet, too linear, too predictable, and there is no coffee or food. They're not open late, either. Traditional libraries are stiff and institutionally predictable, they have sterile architecture, and the chairs are uncomfortable—just like a lot of churches.

FUNDAMENTAL DIFFERENCES

There is a fundamental difference between today's bookstores and yesterday's libraries.

ONE IS DESIGNED FOR experience AND THE OTHER FOR information.

Like libraries, most churches are institutions of modernity and are based on how we thought people learned. When I was a kid, my parents said, "Michael, turn off the television while you're doing homework." So I'd put on my stereo instead. "You can't learn with music blaring," my folks would continue. "Go where it's quiet."

Compare that setting with a phone call I recently made to our son, who is attending an Ivy League college. He's studying for the next day's physics midterm, he's dialoguing with a chat-room group of friends on the Internet, he's playing music in the background, and he's talking to me—all at the same time. Yet he's doing much better in school than I ever hoped for myself!

The lesson: The old method was to minimize noise; today's approach is to multiply stimulation. God made us as multisensory people.

WE LEARN BEST WITH all of our senses ENGAGED.

TOWNS THAT REINVENT THEMSELVES

Small towns are a lot like churches in their need to reinvent themselves for today. In 1999 the last appliance store closed in one of Ohio's county-seat towns near where I live. Its proprietor died, and no one could find a future for the store. Previous closures included the last shoe store and drugstore, both of which had relocated out of the downtown area five years before.

The mayor was convinced that the best solution was to repeat the 1950s. He felt that a replacement store, such as a new drugstore, would draw business back to town. But it hasn't happened.

By contrast my town, Tipp City, with a population of six thousand, continues to reinvent itself. It's now an inviting little community, known for its antique and toy stores, Friday-night music groups on the street (they close the streets and feature music), deli tables on the sidewalks, and an old 1800s hotel that has been turned into a group of specialty shops.

WHILE SOME TOWNS ARE TRYING TO REACH BACK AND GRASP THE PAST, OTHERS MOVE FORWARD TO reinvent themselves FOR THE FUTURE.

Some towns are building a whole new environment for a postmodern experience-economy world.

CHURCHES IN WHICH THE FUTURE IS NOW

Churches are doing that too. My friend Troy Dean pastors University Praise Church in Fullerton, California. He is passionate about multisensory worship that engages the senses as people experience God. It's a far bigger issue than merely adding or removing candles, however. "Candles are not the answer to postmodern experience," he says. "Flow, connection, expression, community, safety, multifaceted learning, participation, activity, space, aesthetics with form, icons, and artifacts—all of these together are what it takes for people to experience God with all their senses engaged."

UnLearning churches realize that people become engaged through environment and experiences. Such churches develop an environment that frees people and allows them to experience God in closer and deeper ways than they've ever experienced before.

This is a spiritual age in which people are looking for an experience of God more than an explanation of God.

TOO MANY PEOPLE BELIEVE THEY CANNOT FIND

an experience of God

IN THE CHURCH.

All they think they'll find in a church are abstract, cerebral ideas; theological definitions; and moral correction.

Jesus is God coming down to earth to serve human needs. The message of the Incarnation is that God comes to everyday people. Like me. Like the church I serve. Like the people in my community who need an experience of God. Churches that reach people today by demonstrating radical Christianity do so by leading people to experience *God*, not *religion.*

Ginghamsburg Church tries each week to help people experience God in a variety of ways. On Christmas Eve, 2000 (which fell on a Sunday), we went farther than we ever had before to help the entire Dayton community have a multisensory experience of God. "We wanted to change Christmas from an event to an experience," explains Kim Miller, Ginghamsburg's creative director. "We wanted people to feel that the heart of their Christmas was the Ginghamsburg experience. So we created a place to bring friends and family to be part of a holiday environment and to interact with others, coming and hanging out for as long as they chose. Our desire was to create a lingering memory of their God-experience that day at Ginghamsburg."

We put flesh on these goals by creating a huge one-stop shop. We had a petting zoo, sleigh rides, a coffee shop featuring a display of works by a local artist, and a jazz band in the foyer. "These gathering points became an oasis that connected us with the awe and wonder of life," says Kim.

And what a day it was! People came in droves, representing almost three times our typical weekend attendance. Not only did Ginghamsburg people bring their friends, but these guests brought *their* friends, too. "We knew that Christmas Eve is still the best day to bring someone to church, so we'd give them the whole nine yards when they came," according to Kim.

Most significant, we introduced something called the Family Room. We used an easily accessible room upstairs from our worship area. It has a cozy atmosphere, couches, candles, and coffee tables. It became a place to meet people to talk over spiritual issues and have prayer. In our fliers that invited people to Christmas Eve, we described all the options available, including the Family Room. (We originally preferred the more user-friendly phrase "Living Room" until we discovered that the term was already in use as the name of a strip club in Dayton.)

At the end of every Worship Celebration, we told people that the Family Room was open and, if they had any needs at all to talk over or pray through, to simply make their way upstairs to the Family Room, where caring and competent people (lay pastors) were waiting to meet with them.

It was a huge success. Even our professional saxophone player from Dayton who had come to play that day kept going up between sets to continue his dialogue with someone in the Family Room.

The Family Room is now an ongoing place of ministry here at Ginghamsburg. We think of it as a postmodern altar or prayer room. The traditional altar experience is challenging here because people can feel herded in and out too quickly, not to mention the lack of privacy in the worship area. We have prayer rooms, but they have space for only one conversation at a time, and most people in our culture find it too intimidating to engage one-on-one with a stranger alone in a small room.

The Family Room was a key piece of our desire to take faith beyond worship. The Christmas Eve atmosphere gave our guests a multisensory environment as a context to experience God afresh.

One Church That's UnLearning

Westwinds Community Church, Jackson, Michigan
www.westwinds.org

QUICK DESCRIPTION: Our vision is to present Christ in a creative, caring, and relationally credible way. We desire to reach the believer as well as the seeker with a message that is as satisfying to their heart as to their head and brings them to maturity in Christ.

HISTORY: nondenominational; started in 1987.

ATTENDANCE: one thousand in three weekend services

THEME: Learning Best by Engaging All Our Senses

WHAT THE LEADER SAYS: "We're unLearning the amount of anonymity and space desired by our guests. Lost people usually want connection and answers or they wouldn't be showing up. They find it very compelling when they authentically connect with God in worship, especially when we involve all their senses.

"For example, in one service about brokenness, we had lots going on simultaneously: lighting, visual art, scent, hearing, and touch. The room was set up so 'experiencers' saw a large pile of broken tile as they entered. The lighting was in earthy oranges, browns, and burgundies, accented by more than a hundred candles (tea lights) and candelabra. A scent was in the air from rosemary oil atomizers. TV monitors showed images of deep sadness, tragedy, and brokenness. The huge center screen displayed digital art with the word *restoration*. In front of the low stage was a pool of water lined with rocks and broken pieces of tile.

"The service began with a line from a popular song, 'I feel so broken I don't know if I will ever get put back together again.' Participants were given their own piece of broken tile. A poetic reading, interspersed with readings from Psalm 51, walked them into a reflection on their own need for restoration.

"Worshippers then had multiple options for response. They could receive Communion, laying their broken tile at the feet of a digital crucifix. They could go to an anointing station for prayers of restoration. Or they could float tea candles in a large pool in front of the stage, symbolizing a need to reconnect to Jesus, who, as Light of the World, can show his light on our interior space and heal our woundedness. Some wanted to experience all three options."

—*Ron Martoia, transformational architect and brain juice hydrant, has pastored the church since the beginning; age mid-thirties.*

How Are **you** UnLearning?

- What is one thing you are unLearning so that people can better engage their senses and experience God?

- What senses other than hearing will you use to help your people enjoy your times together?

Inviting Innovation and Change

People today are looking beyond meetings—they yearn for meaning. UnLearning churches have shifted the emphasis from quantity to quality and from church growth to church health. They engage people through personal interaction, not doctrinal ideology.

Being in Christ is about quality of life, not quantity of life. Jesus did not say, "I came that you may have more stuff" or "I came that you may be elevated to higher positions." Jesus said, "I came that they [those who belong to him] may have life, and have it abundantly" (John 10:10b).

You and I yearn for meaning. We want our lives to count. God has woven into our beings a desire to pursue significance. We are wired for it. Yet even followers of Jesus can become so quickly distracted that we trade significance for temporal success.

JESUS SAID GREATNESS IS
who God is making you to be,
NOT HOW MUCH YOU HAVE.

Jesus' disciples had to unLearn their definition of greatness.

One day Jesus' close followers, Peter, James, and John, began arguing over which of them would be the most important. They had just returned from a mountaintop retreat with Jesus. They had experienced the power of God, and now, just a day later, were already being overcome with an exaggerated sense of their own importance. They were confusing self-centered success with God-centered purpose.

"When Jesus realized how much this mattered to them, he brought a child to his side" (Luke 9:47, *The Message*). What is true greatness? " 'Whoever accepts this child as if the child were me, accepts me,' he said. 'And whoever accepts me, accepts the One who sent me' " (Luke 9:48a, *The Message*).

"You become great by accepting, not asserting," Jesus said. Not grabbing, not controlling, not manipulating. "Your spirit, not your size, makes the difference," Jesus concluded (Luke 9:48b, *The Message*).

TAKE TWO PILLS AND FIND LIFE'S MEANING

Even when we pursue God's meaning in life, we sometimes think it can come instantly and with no work.

WE ARE CREATED TO REFLECT A maturity
THAT COMES FROM GOD.

(See Ephesians 4:13.) Even though a lot of Jesus' followers try to get through life on a pass-fail basis, at a deep level we don't enjoy mediocrity. We long to be better than average. We want to achieve a higher level for the honor and purpose of God—not for our own personal success but achievement with excellence for the purpose of reflecting God's honor and purpose.

Our culture is drawn toward impulse living. We've all seen advertisements for diet supplements. They claim dramatic change almost instantly. Television regularly hawks testimonials of people saying "I lost sixty pounds in three months" or "I developed a muscle-toned, athletic look in forty-two days."

WE ARE TEMPTED TO GO THE ROUTE OF
easy rather than right,
SO WE BUY INTO THESE WISHFUL CLAIMS.

We want it to be magic. We don't want to have to work. We convince ourselves that we'll become different by taking a pill or drinking a high-nutrition formula.

The most ridiculous advertisement I've seen is the one that promotes audiotapes: "Learn to speak Spanish in your sleep." I want to believe that when the audiotapes arrive in my mailbox, I'll receive help in speaking Spanish merely by carrying them into my house and putting them in a tape player.

You are not going to become the person God created you to be just by listening to tapes or simply wanting to find your God-destiny. Faith is work. Finding God's meaning for your life requires a process of personal transformation.

THE POWER BEHIND INNOVATION AND CHANGE

A culture that seeks to fill the spiritual vacuum left by the cult of scientific materialism can easily become unbalanced in its quest. UnLearning churches keep the focus on human worth, health, and personal relationships. The result is this:

UNLEARNING CHURCHES ARE INCREDIBLE ATMOSPHERES OF

innovation and change.

Life transformation, not church growth, becomes the measure of success.

People often make resolutions after a holiday, and especially at the beginning of every new year. Diet is always one of the big resolutions. But life-change is about a lot more. Change and transformation go much deeper than resolutions that deal with diets, debt, and addictions.

We will never experience lasting change in our lives if we are operating out of motivations that begin with the word *should*. Shoulds are not a powerful enough motivational force to bring lasting change.

At one point I tried my hardest to go on a low-fat diet. I was successful for all of three weeks. Living out of resolutions for what I *should* do lacks sustaining power. The solution is living out of call.

BELIEVING THAT WE HAVE HEARD

the voice of God

CHANGES "SHOULD DO" INTO "MUST DO."

We learn to live out of call when we begin to think and act with God.

We must come to the place of power that is beyond willpower. All of a sudden *should* becomes *must*. When we're living out of must, we find God's power to change. That transition is the ultimate makeover. Other people will look at us and see a holistic force that is bigger than we are.

Jesus was intimately aware of the presence of God. As Jesus was praying, thinking, and walking close to God, "the appearance of his face changed" (Luke 9:29). This same experience happened to other people in the Bible as well. "Moses did not know that the skin of his face shone because he had been talking with God" (Exodus 34:29b). (See also 2 Corinthians 3:7-11.)

PEOPLE LOOKED AT HIM AND SAW THE reflection

OF GOD'S PRESENCE.

The same thing can happen with you. As people see God in you, they will become more aware of God. They will notice God's hope and possibilities for their own lives. It's exciting when God's life oozes out through you, touches other

people, and makes other people's lives better. That's living. That's a life of innovation and change.

QUALITY OVER QUANTITY

In their atmospheres of innovation and change, unLearning churches focus on *quality* of experience rather than *quantity* of people. Success is not measured in numbers alone; it's about transformed lives.

Thousands of churches in the 1980s and 1990s focused on a barrier-breaking model. Popular conferences offered the management techniques needed to work with larger groups of people. Smaller churches tried to break the two hundred barrier, and larger churches learned how to grow through the thousand barrier.

Too many churches used those calibrations to concentrate more on quantity than quality.

TOO MANY OF US

measured our success

BY THE NUMBER OF PEOPLE IN ATTENDANCE.

The unLearning church doesn't fixate on how it can grow toward human standards of greatness. It's preoccupied instead with how to be in the life-transformation business. Its leaders would jump at a chance to take on a community of one hundred radical followers of Jesus rather than a minimum-commitment crowd of several thousand.

At Ginghamsburg we've learned that sometimes our shifts to higher quality have cost us quantity. In 2000, we phased out one of our Saturday night services so we could offer a talkback time after the 5:25 worship celebration. For those in attendance, this met a real need for personal interaction that led to life change on their part. This strategic focus created time restraints. It prevented us from leading a second celebration later that evening.

We did what promoted life change, not what made the most business sense to gather the largest crowds. We committed ourselves to the real business of Jesus—life transformation—and not to the sometimes superficial business of church growth.

By today's standards,

JESUS' THREE-YEAR EXPERIENCE WITH HIS DISCIPLES

WOULD BE CONSIDERED A FAILURE.

At the end of Jesus' earthly ministry, he had only 120 people in his church. No one today would pay to go to Jesus' church-growth seminar. Who would come? From outward appearances, it would not appear to be a model of success.

Instead of emphasizing quantity of people, he focused on quality of growth. Jesus had three years to build a ministry, and his approach was to focus on twelve people, one of whom failed miserably. JESUS ministered to THE MULTITUDE, BUT HE majored on THE TWELVE DISCIPLES. When he left planet Earth, his church had 120 people. Yet Jesus' church of 120 high-impact leaders turned the world upside down.

You and I are following Christ today because of the depth Jesus built into a small number of people. How are you and I doing likewise?

UnLearning Moment

What views about the church do you need to unLearn to develop a new standard for measuring success? What new standard can you develop for measuring success in your church?

HEALTH OVER SIZE

UnLearning churches focus more on church *health* than on church *growth*. Healthy organisms grow naturally. Churches that are healthy tend to grow in size.

For any organization to create change, it needs a radical product. The church's radical product is revolutionary people—real followers of Jesus Christ, which I describe in a previous book, *Real Followers: Beyond Virtual Christianity* (Abingdon, 1999). As churches take seriously Jesus' call to discipleship, their memberships change from consumer mindsets to mission-outreach movements of God whose members demonstrate both personal and social holiness.

When I used to hear the word *church*, I thought of something innocuous, boring, and bland. Christianity was "nice-ianity." Then I began to look into the book of Acts. I discovered that Christianity is anything but nice. It is extreme. There are no middles. Everywhere these people went, either revolutions or riots occurred. It was radical.

Radical church is not a place; it is a people. You really can't say, "I'm going to church." Church is a gathering, a collection of people called together and called out. We are unique. We possess a common heart and a common mind. We have a passion to do things for Jesus.

THE MOST INCREDIBLE EXPERIENCE OF OUR LIVES IS THAT WE GET TO BE

servants of God.

I recently watched a movement spring up at Ginghamsburg. It is a group of young heroes from ages eighteen to thirty. They've named themselves The Gathering. These are young people with a sense of being called out and together. They talk with one another about where their mission needs to go. Then they make it happen as they mentor others in their age group. They exemplify what it means to be one in heart and passion.

Radical church

IS THE *POWER* OF GOD DEMONSTRATED THROUGH OUR COMMON LIFE TOGETHER.

We are changed by the ways we live in relationship.

Programs and events do not change people. You and I can place expectations on each other that don't belong on people but belong on God. We look to each other to be perfect, and only God is perfect. When we put that kind of unrealistic expectation on people, it creates disillusionment with one another. Our misplaced expectations cause us to withhold our life force from one another.

Radical church is God's *prototype* of an authentic community. We do not expect perfection from one another. Only God can give that. We look to one another to experience grace, encouragement, and accountability. We can encourage one another to become all that Christ has created us to be.

The human body is a unit. Though it is made up of many parts, they form one body. So it is with Christ. For we were all baptized by one Spirit into one body— whether Jews or Greeks; slave or free; old or young; rich or poor; black, white, yellow, or brown. We were all given one Spirit. (See Galatians 3:27-28 and 1 Corinthians 12:12-13.)

THAT'S WHAT RADICAL CHURCH LOOKS LIKE.

Not a place, but a people.

NOT A PROGRAM, BUT A POWER. NOT A PRETENSE,
BUT A PROTOTYPE OF authentic community.

How does a place like Ginghamsburg get beyond virtual Christianity—something that looks like the real deal from the outside but is actually only a facade? I never left the church I came to back in 1979. It had ninety people with a $27,000 annual budget. The community of Ginghamsburg is a couple dozen houses. It's so small that it doesn't show up on most maps. Our church campus is three miles from Tipp City, with a population of six thousand. We're sixteen miles north of Dayton, Ohio, which has 180,000 people. You have to drive a twenty-five-mile radius around Dayton before you will find one million people.

What did we do to grow a healthy church in that setting? We invited people to our home, exposed them to the book of Acts, modeled the idea of taking Jesus at his word and reaching out to others, and challenged these people to do likewise. Of 35,000 United Methodist churches, Ginghamsburg is in the top ten in terms of worship attendance.[1] Ginghamsburg has become a hub of life-change by the power of the Holy Spirit, with ripple effects around the world!

I TRACE OUR HEALTH AND GROWTH TO A
radical focus ON JESUS CHRIST.

Jesus was not into building programs, technology, media, or megachurches. He was about the business of empowering people to seek the lost, strengthen the weak, heal the sick, bind up the injured, and bring back those who had strayed. Not a program, but a radical demonstration of the power of God.

MEANING OVER ACTIVITY

UnLearning churches focus more on connecting people to *meaning* than to *activity*. Ten years ago we would have emphasized getting people to show up for church programs and listen-and-learn meetings. We would have sponsored a seminar and gauged its success by how many attended.

Today people are not looking for church *meetings* so much as for life *meaning*.

NOW WE MEASURE SUCCESS BY ASKING,
"HOW ARE PEOPLE FINDING life change AND purpose
THROUGH THE EXPERIENCE?"

Does it make a difference in their relationships, parenting skills, Christian witness, and stewardship?

This paradigm translates to the organization's structure as well. Older-mindset churches usually require a lot of committees and meetings. Ginghamsburg finds that its people have neither the time nor the patience for multiple committee activities, so we are down to one committee of nine people called the Leadership Board (to be explained more in chapters 15 and 16). No more staff-parish, missions, or finance committees. Major businesses operate with one board, but too often tiny churches have become immobilized by layers of committees.

RELATIONSHIP OVER IDEOLOGY

UnLearning churches focus more on *relationship* than *ideology*. Like Velcro, these churches excel in offering multiple places to stick and connect. They encourage interaction and help people connect with one another. They build leaders shaped by the values of the movement, and the leaders in turn build people.

We must make the development of leaders the highest priority. The potential of the movement is in the development of the leadership. Programs don't attract a following; people do. If you add leaders, your movement multiplies. It takes leaders to raise up more leaders.

THE LEADER'S JOB IS TO

build the people

WHO WILL BUILD THE MOVEMENT.

That's why Jesus spent so much time in prayer and in person with the twelve people who would lead the movement.

In its early days, the modern-day church growth movement gave the impression that growing churches were homogenous groupings where everyone was (or should be) alike. The idea of "homogeneous units" gave the impression that everyone in a church would sport the same skin color, economic status, and political persuasion.

There is a big problem with that value.

"PEOPLE-JUST-LIKE-ME" CHURCHES

ARE unlike THE KINGDOM OF GOD.

The ideology of what works best culturally is sometimes an anathema to the kingdom of God. God envisions people from "every tribe and language and people and nation" (Revelation 5:9b) who are worshipping together.

The Apostle Paul warns us, "Has not God made foolish the wisdom of the world?" (1 Corinthians 1:20b). The church as the prototype community of God presses us beyond our comfort zones. Part of my job is to afflict the comfortable—and I see a lot of comfortable people in most church gatherings!

A lot of us think faith is something that is supposed to make us comfortable. We think we should go to church and gain a sense of peace. If all we want is peace, we could find our way to a beach, park, or spa.

Walking with God is not about being comfortable or finding the easy life. The follower of Jesus does not live in the middle. We live out on the edge, in total dependence on God.

Being a real follower of Jesus is not about comfort. It's not about blending into the crowd. Followers of Jesus make the declaration, "Here I stand. If I perish, I perish, but I must do the will of God for my life." Whatever lies ahead almost doesn't matter because Jesus is there, and he is everything we want and everything we need.

When I'm comfortable, I stay in the same places. But Jesus wants me to welcome his innovation and change in my life.

One Church That's UnLearning

Spirit Garage (a church with a *really* big door), uptown Minneapolis, Minnesota
www.spiritgarage.org

QUICK DESCRIPTION: Committed to reaching deeper in relationship with Christ, growing larger in outreach to people in transition, growing closer in genuine community, and reaching wider in service to the "least of these."

HISTORY: Lutheran (ELCA); started in 1997.

ATTENDANCE: 150 in two Sunday-morning services

THEME: Beyond Membership

WHAT THE LEADER SAYS: "The foremost thing I've had to unLearn is the tendency to try too quickly to define what God is doing in the congregation. Sometimes what looks like failure is in fact just a call to reconsider how we should proceed with the opportunities that God is presenting us.

"The biggest example is church membership. Dozens of people are active, committed, giving, serving, and worshipping but have no interest in 'official' membership. Also, those who are on the fringes, for whatever reasons, still play a big part in making this community what it is.

"In the end we've chosen a both-and approach. We offer a membership covenant and traditional new-member orientations. If pushed, we give those as our official membership numbers. But practically speaking, our active worship attendees are a much more accurate guide to who is part of this community and who is committed. We'll never overemphasize the signing of a piece of paper (or even worse, agreeing to a set of 'minimum requirements') at the expense of taking focus away from the ongoing growth and giving we have come to see and expect from people who get involved here."

—*Pam Fickensher, pastor, has been with the church since its beginning; age early thirties.*

How Are **you** UnLearning?

• What must the leaders in your church live without so that they can be more receptive to Jesus' innovations and changes in their lives?

• Imagine a metaphor or symbol for a healthy church: "A healthy church is like…" Draw your symbol.

ENDNOTES

1. John Vaughan, "Top 100," *Almanac of the Christian World* (Tyndale, 1992), 361-363.

Safe Space to Ask Hard Questions

UnLearning churches offer an environment of trust.
They value a climate of safe space where people can ask
honest questions. They don't feel compelled to give all
the right answers.

Jesus understood the power of great questions.

When he was twelve, his parents found him in the temple, "sitting among the teachers, listening to them and asking them questions" (Luke 2:46). When he began his public ministry, he constantly asked questions of his disciples. "How many loaves have you?" he asked before involving them in the miracle of feeding more than five thousand people from seven loaves and a few small fish. (See Matthew 15:34.) Even at the trial that led to his death, Jesus answered his critics with questions. "Then Pilate entered the headquarters again, summoned Jesus, and asked him, 'Are you the King of the Jews?' Jesus answered, 'Do you ask this on your own, or did others tell you about me?' " (John 18:33-34).

The church of my childhood was consumed with giving the right answers.

CHURCHES OF TOMORROW FOCUS ON ASKING
the right questions.

What was Jesus' most-used method of teaching? Asking questions of his followers.

People like me want clear answers. If I had been alive during Jesus' earthly ministry, I would have pressed him hard to get the inside scoop on who he was. "Come on, Jesus," I'd have said, "I have my notebook open and pen ready. Please cut to the chase and tell me who you are."

But Jesus answered questions with questions: "Who do *you* say that I am?" (Matthew 16:15, emphasis added).

John the Baptist struggled when he was in jail. He asked questions of the faith he had once proclaimed with confidence. He sent his students to Jesus to ask,

"Are you really the one we are waiting for, or shall we keep on looking?" (Matthew 11:3, TLB). Jesus didn't give him the exact answer he might have been looking for. Nor did Jesus promise to get him out of jail. He simply said, "Go back to John and tell him about the miracles you've seen me do—the blind people I've healed, and the lame people now walking without help, and the cured lepers, and the deaf who hear, and the dead raised to life; and tell him about my preaching the Good News to the poor" (Matthew 11:4-5, TLB).

GROWTH COMES BY ASKING

We think life could be easier if we could only receive clear and immediate answers.

JESUS UNDERSTOOD THAT REAL GROWTH HAPPENS as we struggle WITH SIGNIFICANT QUESTIONS, when we can have the safe emotional space to do so without judgment. If people aren't free to ask hard questions, they may never get the real answers they need.

I'M unLearning THE HABIT OF GIVING QUICK ANSWERS.

I asked Sherry Douglas, who directed our children's ministries at Ginghamsburg for many years, how many questions the average child asks in an average day. She estimated more than one hundred. Some parents would say their toddlers ask three hundred a day!

By the time we're middle-age adults, the average is down to a handful of significant questions a day. As we grow older, we have a tendency to lose our inquiring sense of awe and wonder. We forget how to be childlike. We quit asking questions.

unLearning Moment

Name one way you are unLearning your preoccupation with answers. What is one evidence in your life that questions are becoming more important to you?

CHURCHES AS ENVIRONMENTS OF TRUST

An unLearning church becomes an environment of trust. UnLearning churches create safe spaces where the Spirit can work through people's inquiring quests for God. They welcome people who don't give or have all the "right" answers. They invite people to ask honest questions without chastising folks for struggling with the answers.

How am I going to tell you what to believe when I don't have all the answers? I was once spiritually blind. Jesus opened my eyes and made me see. He was resurrected from the grave and changed my life. But there are many days when I still pray, "I believe; help my unbelief." In fact, it's one of my frequent prayers.

I'm not the only church leader who needs safe space to be honest like that. When I watch other leaders offer that level of transparency in the questions they're asking, I begin to see authenticity in their lives. They become credible. If they are credible, then what they believe becomes authentic to me.

The desire for safe space is not limited to church leaders. In her book *Traveling Mercies: Some Thoughts on Faith*, Anne Lamott describes how she found a church that was a safe place for her. As you experience the narrative of her life journey, with its earthy language, painful failures, and times of confusion and disillusionment, you become convinced that she is for real. She has invited the God of Jesus Christ to invade her life, and she credits her church as a people who accepted her when she was pregnant and unwed, as a place that continues to welcome her to ask hard questions.

My friend Scott Parsons, on a similar journey but a different road, makes connections for me. In 1998, at age fifty-one, he came to Ginghamsburg. During his third year with us, he made a faith commitment to be a Jesus follower. He did this in a community that's striving to connect people to an experience of God, that lives in paradox, and that provides a safe environment to ask critical questions.

Here's what Scott says about his Jesus journey:

I guess I'm still a seeker and always will be—but by way of a very convoluted path, I have come to a point of referring to myself as "tentatively Christian." I got to this point by translating the essential vocabulary of Christians into meanings I could embrace. It has worked well enough that now I rarely feel the need to translate.

When I think of a church setting out to make an appeal to a seeker like me—knowing my own attitudes and resistances—I'm very impressed that they'd even try. It seems to me like what they're doing is similar to adopting children who have highly limiting and irreversible challenges and conditions—the kind only a miracle can overcome.

For people like me, actions completely drown out words. Behavior—Christian behavior—is the only thing that will win us. There's nothing more persuasive in the human range of acts.

A brave "seeker church" operates on the certainty that God is much too great to be threatened by a seeker's wild questions or unconventional speculation. It wasn't arguments that ultimately made God real for me. I think it was the gradual turning of my attention toward God—something that happened because of Ginghamsburg Church. I had to be listening to hear God.

As a seeker, what have I been seeking? It has never been salvation or heaven. I'm not really interested in those wonderful gifts, although I won't refuse them if they are offered. What I wanted was an encounter with a real God, someone who can take me higher.

That encounter began for me one ordinary day when my mind was relaxed and I suddenly realized that I knew that God was present around me.

As for Jesus, I am still seeking to understand him. I place faith in the idea that if I love Jesus enough, belief will fall to the side. And I do love Jesus.

Scott Parsons is someone who asks lots of questions, and I hear God through Scott's life. Scott came to Ginghamsburg as a self-described agnostic, although his attendance has been better than that of many members. After a long period of critical questioning in a safe environment, he declared that he is a tentative follower of Jesus. Still in process.

WHICH GOD TO BELIEVE IN?

People today believe in God. This is not an anti-god culture. They believe in God, gods, and goddesses—they just don't know which one.

IT'S THE FIRST TIME IN AMERICAN HISTORY THAT A spiritual awakening IS BEING LED BY MOVEMENTS OTHER THAN THE CHRISTIAN CHURCH.

Today's post-Christian spirituality is one that rejects absolutes and intolerance. It is a spirituality with no biblical concepts. It sees Christianity's claim of exclusiveness as unacceptable—part of a closed worldview. Yet Jesus said, "I am the way, and the truth, and the life. No one comes to the Father except through me" (John 14:6). The early church affirmed that "there is no other name under heaven given among mortals by which we must be saved" (Acts 4:12b).

Jesus' motive in teaching was not so that we could argue others into becoming his followers. Jesus said, "I am giving you these commands so that you may love one another" (John 15:17). That kind of environment becomes a safe place for people to ask questions and grow.

Love is the essence of who God is. The Bible says God is love. (See 1 John 4:8, 16.)

Love today can mean anything from "I love the taste of chocolate cake" to "I love the adrenaline-surge of roller coasters" to "I get goose bumps when I talk with you." Jesus clarifies his meaning of love when he says, in effect, "This is what I mean by love. When you love, love others as I have loved you." (See John 15:12.)

How did Jesus love us? He was physically present. Though he existed in the form of God, he set that aside and pitched his tent right where we live. (See John 1:14.) He modeled the importance of physical presence, of appropriate touch, and of the relationship between healing and wholeness.

Jesus also showed love by his emotional honesty. He displayed an attitude that exhibited a huge emotional connection to his followers. "I do not call you servants any longer, because the servant does not know what the master is doing; but I have called you friends, because I have made known to you everything that I have heard from my Father" (John 15:15). If we are only physically present but not emotionally available, we are treating those around us like they are servants.

Emotional honesty involves being in touch with and aware of what is happening inside of me. If I am not aware of that, I will be physically present but emotionally unavailable. This can lead to emotional and even physical abuse.

AT HOME IN JESUS' LOVE

Jesus said, "Make yourselves at home in my love" (John 15:7, *The Message*). You are secure and strong in being who God created you to be. Your identity is shaped by the Lord Jesus, not by those around you.

Can you imagine a people who live in an environment of grace and unconditional love? A safe-space environment like that would encourage us to be honest enough to work on our stuff. It would give us the freedom to tell the truth of who we really are on the inside.

When I move out of fear and into this place of trust, I begin to truly live. I make a difference in God's created purpose.

EMERGING CHURCHES ARE

communities of grace-space

THAT ALLOW SEEKERS THE FREEDOM TO DEAL WITH THEIR HEART QUESTIONS.

One Church That's UnLearning

The Meeting House, Oakville, Ontario, Canada
www.themeetinghouse.ca

QUICK DESCRIPTION: A church for people who aren't into church, experimental in format while staying fiercely biblical in content.

HISTORY: Brethren in Christ; started 1986.

ATTENDANCE: 1000+

THEME: Making Time for "Q & Eh?"

WHAT THE LEADER SAYS: "We include a question-and-answer period as part of our Sunday teaching time each week. In today's culture we're encouraged to ask questions in grade school, high school, college, and university, but then we invite people to learn at church and expect them to be quiet, passive receivers of truth.

"Our ongoing challenge is to find ways of keeping our Sunday services open and interactive even as numbers grow. Our 'Q & Eh?' time (we're Canadians) is the part of the sermon that many people most look forward to and tell others about."

—Bruxy Cavey, pastor, has been with the church since 1996; age late thirties.

How Are **you** UnLearning?

- What are some times you have experienced being safe in your church?

- What honest questions do you imagine people in your community want to ask?

- How are you building a climate of safe space for people to ask honest questions? What are you unLearning in order to get there?

8 A Culture of Reckless Love

The world doesn't need religious organizations but communities that demonstrate Christ's reckless love. UnLearning churches guide people along their spiritual journeys by demonstrating authentic lifestyles of reckless love.

When Jesus first met some of his potential disciples, he found them fishing close to the shore. Shallow waters are safe and predictable. Shoreline work is logical and risk-free.

As Jesus spoke with them about their fishing tactics, he was in essence saying to them, "You will never become who God created you to be if you hang out here where it is safe and predictable. If you are going to maximize this incredible gift of life that God has given you, you have to cast out to dangerous places. You've got to go out there to the deep spots." (See Luke 5:1-11.)

What does it mean to be a follower of Jesus? It requires a lifestyle of potential unpredictability, out in deeper waters. Yet we spend most of our lives working hard to keep life safe and controlled.

That's how many of our parents in the post-World War II generation define success. Getting ahead in life, we learned, is about working hard to create security and comfort with minimal risk.

People today find ways to make a living, but we don't know how to live. There is a big difference between the two!

We do the same thing with religion. We want gods we can tame and define—who will make life safe and predictable. So we come up with little gods that fit into nice, neat categories.

I AM UNLEARNING THE IDEA THAT *safe* IS BEST.

People grow the most in times of tension, adversity, and crisis. That's why my spiritual intent at Ginghamsburg is to be a source of irritation to lives that are

safe and predictable. We don't grow when we're comfortable. A pearl is formed from a grain of sand that becomes the irritant in the shell of an oyster.

CLEAN, EASY EXPLANATIONS WON'T DO

When our daughter, Kristen, was young, she came home from school one day and told me she had learned about bees. "God made the bees, and Satan made the stinger," she said. Isn't that a nice, neat explanation? It puts our minds at ease, but life isn't really that simple.

Life is complex, and so is God. God isn't tame. Predictability and faith cannot coexist. They're opposites. They cannot be in the same place at the same time.

Jesus was a lawbreaker. He did everything that you weren't supposed to do. Mark 2:1–3:6 gives a snapshot description of Jesus' unpredictability. He didn't fit the definition of what religious people thought he ought to be. He ate at the wrong houses. He hung out with prostitutes, thieves, and scoundrels. He broke religious rules. He didn't fit into people's simplistic equations of what religion was supposed to look like.

Jesus would more likely be accepted today by an audience on the Oprah show than by most people in today's churches. That's why he was rejected. He didn't fit into the religious categories of a safe Messiah.

People quickly saw that Jesus would disrupt their normal life patterns.

Does it ever amaze you that Jesus would go into some town and pull off an amazing miracle and then people would ask him to leave? If Jesus stayed around, it would disrupt the social, religious, and economic scope of things. He'd do things like curse a fig tree or turn over the moneychangers' tables. Who would let this man influence their children? If Jesus came into our communities today, he wouldn't pass most churches' requirements to teach children's Sunday school.

Jesus calls us to leave safe places.

PUSHED INTO THE WILD

Notice what happened abruptly after Jesus' baptism. The Spirit immediately pushed Jesus out into the wild. "And the Spirit immediately drove him out into the wilderness. He was in the wilderness forty days, tempted by Satan; and he was with the wild beasts; and the angels waited on him" (Mark 1:12-13). The

Spirit that on an earlier occasion appeared as a safe dove now forced Jesus out into the wild where doves are replaced by vultures. Satan and wild beasts became Jesus' companions, yet angels protected him.

Imagine two people who find themselves in a room filled with manure. One of them immediately begins to look for a way out. The other asks for a shovel because he knows that in the middle of all that manure, there's bound to be a pony somewhere!

During Jesus' forty wilderness days and nights, Satan tested him, and wild animals were his companions. Jesus knew there was a "pony" in there somewhere: Angels were tending him and caring for him.

When Carolyn and I took our son, Jonathan, for campus visits at colleges that were talking to him about baseball scholarships, we stayed at local motels. Jonathan went off to live with the baseball players to find out what campus life was like. When we would see him the next morning, he always looked thoroughly tired.

At one place he stayed up until 3:00 in the morning. I asked him if students were doing a lot of drinking, and he said, "Yep, it's amazing. There were four kegs of beer for the legs of a Ping-Pong table." I asked him if they stocked any soft drinks or other alternatives to alcohol. "No, all they had was beer," he said. He spoke about one girl who had passed out, and how he had to make sure she was OK. She was only drunk, but there was vomit everywhere.

I told Jonathan, "This is what we prepared you for.

LIFE IS not about staying IN THE SAFE PLACES.

Ginghamsburg has been a good place for you to grow up, but now you're getting kicked out. You were baptized and you took mission trips. Now God will take you out, and wild beasts will be your companions. Jonathan, these dangerous places are the space where we proclaim and demonstrate the good news of God."

TOO MUCH DULLNESS IN CHURCH

We were thankful that our son looked at secular universities because our daughter went to a Christian university that was full of dullness. I don't want my children to be dull in church, in school, or in life. The same principle applies at our churches, which too often have a reputation for dullness.

WE ARE followers of Jesus Christ WHO WALKED OUT OF THE GRAVE.

Life in Jesus is passionate living! People should be tearing down the door to get next to us.

One of the schools we took Jonathan to was an Ivy League college. All the baseball players kept talking about the "Mormon kid." This young man from Cincinnati, a follower of the Mormon faith, had started on the baseball team in his freshman year and had the potential to be drafted into professional baseball.

Then he left his Ivy League education and the opportunity to fulfill his life's dream in baseball. He gave it all up to go to Seoul, Korea, for two years as a missionary, as required by his church.

I had a chance to meet him, so I asked, "What did you have to do when you went to Korea for two years? I took my son there once for ten days."

"I learned Korean so that I could witness to them," he replied.

"Did you do it out of your heart or because it is an expected thing that every Mormon kid from nineteen to twenty-one does?" I asked.

"Oh, no," he said. "Some kids who grow up in the Mormon Church go on mission because it's the expected thing, but I did it out of my heart."

I thought to myself, "Wow! People of other faith backgrounds have much to teach us about the passionate nature of a 'godly' relationship."

PASSION VS. DULLNESS

Carolyn, Jonathan, and I were passing through Chicago's O'Hare Airport, and we bumped into my friend Tim Celek, who wrote *Inside the Soul of a New Generation*. His Gen-X congregation in southern California's Newport Beach is building a facility that's based on the architectural style of a House of Blues restaurant and bar. We spoke for a while and then headed different directions to catch our planes; ours for home, and his for a speaking engagement.

All of a sudden, I stopped and yelled down the concourse, "Celek!" This was a Thursday night in a full airport, and Carolyn began to look embarrassed. I yelled again, "Celek, be sure to lift up Jesus!" And he yelled back, "I will!"

I can't keep from showing this kind of passion! What Jesus has done in my life is simply amazing.

GOD WANTS TO CREATE A

passionate tension IN OUR LIVES,

A HOLY DISCOMFORT.

UnLearning Moment

What is one way you have recently created a moment of holy discomfort at church? What have you needed to unLearn in the process?

So many of us die unfulfilled. Life is about whole living. We think with our minds, and most of us never get past that stage. We try to have a relationship with God in our minds. We claim to have a faith walk with God, but it's only a mind walk that's calculated, careful, and rational.

Sometimes it seems that the greatest distance in the universe is the distance from my mind to my heart. Jesus needs to reach my heart so he can lead me to a place of passionate heart living.

UNLEARNING TO CREATE TENSION

WHEN YOU BECOME infected by the risen Christ,

YOU WILL CREATE A TENSION IN YOUR SURROUNDING CULTURE.

You can't help it. You might be in the middle of Chicago's O'Hare Airport—or at church! You will make people uncomfortable with the unpredictable presence of Jesus Christ.

Where do we grow? In places of tension, in places of conflict, and in places of discomfort—it is in those places that we begin to ask stretching kinds of questions again. Otherwise we form little comfortable gods in our own image, and we follow and believe a nice, safe, tame Jesus.

If we still have the same understanding of Jesus we had twenty years ago, we're probably not growing. God is unchanging. God is the same yesterday, today, and tomorrow (see Hebrews 13:8), but our understanding and discovery of God grows and deepens. This maturity happens if we allow ourselves to remain in places of discomfort.

John the Baptizer asked Jesus if he was the one they were looking for. Jesus said, in essence, "I am, but I am not going to open the door of your prison or your uncomfortable place." (See Matthew 11:2-6.)

A lot of us want the Jesus of our imagination to deliver us from uncomfortable

91

places. The message of Jesus to John was to have courage. "Trust me. It is me. I will be with you always, even in the middle of the crap. I am the pony. I am with you always, even in death."

John never left prison. He was beheaded. Following Jesus cost him his life. What is the word for Jonathan when he goes to a place that is one constant drunk house? "Courage! Remember who you are and whose you are."

NOT SAFE, BUT GOOD

Spiritual life is beyond logical belief. It is an intuitive relationship. "The Holy Spirit will come upon you," the angel told Mary, mother of Jesus (Luke 1:35). I don't understand that. "The power of the Most High will overshadow you," the angel continued. It is not about understanding; it's not about believing; it is an intuitive relationship.

C.S. Lewis was an atheist who taught at Oxford and Cambridge Universities, in England. He found a relationship with Christ through his friend, writer J.R.R. Tolkien.[1] Lewis then wrote a series of books called *The Chronicles of Narnia*. In these fairy tales, Lewis tries to explain what it would look like if God entered the world. In his story, Jesus is a lion by the name of Aslan who comes to the mythical land of Narnia.

In the second book of the series, *The Lion, the Witch and the Wardrobe*, four children from England magically entered Narnia, and they first heard about Aslan from Mr. and Mrs. Beaver. They were frightened to learn that he was a lion, and they asked if he was tame. The character Susan said, "I shall feel rather nervous about meeting a lion."

" 'That you will, dearie, and no mistake,' said Mrs. Beaver, 'if there's anyone who can appear before Aslan without their knees knocking, they're either braver than most or else just silly.'

" 'Then he isn't safe?' said Lucy.

" 'Safe?' said Mr. Beaver. 'Don't you hear what Mrs. Beaver tells you?...'Course he isn't safe. But he's good. He's the King.' "

Too many Christians today are dull and sleepy because we have made Jesus, the Lion of Judah, safe, predictable, and logical. Lions aren't tame. We think we know what will happen next, but you can't pin Jesus down. He's not predictable.

Nor will churches be predictable as they follow Jesus. Just when our people think Ginghamsburg is predictable, God throws a curve. But God does it for a reason.

You don't know what will happen next because following Jesus is not about

God-talk. It's about God-breath. The God-talker depends on safe and predictable outcomes.

THE GOD-BREATHER EXPECTS

surprise endings.

The God-talker is controlled by guidelines. The God-breather lives by a relationship, not rules. The God-talker likes to know what to expect. God-breathers know they must stay in touch with the Spirit to know the real deal. God-talkers need plans and structure. The God-breather is fluid and spontaneous.

LIVES TURNED INSIDE OUT

THE EMERGING CHURCH IS FOR PEOPLE

WHO WANT THEIR LIVES

turned inside out

BY THE LIVING GOD.

"As the Father has loved me, so I have loved you; abide in my love" (John 15:9). Jesus' command doesn't say anything about belief. "If you keep my commandments, you will abide in my love, just as I have kept my Father's commandments and abide in his love" (John 15:10). What determines the actions in your life? Your passions. Passions are tied to your ultimate love, not your intellectual beliefs.

Jesus continues, "I have said these things to you so that my joy may be in you, and that your joy may be complete" (John 15:11). Religion doesn't have anything to do with joy. Passion has everything to do with joy. Jesus concludes, "This is my commandment, that you love one another as I have loved you" (John 15:12).

Jesus is calling your church and my church not to religious belief but to an affair of the heart. Jesus invites us into an intimate, passionate relationship.

This world doesn't need another institutional religion that goes out and tells people what to do. What Jesus is building and putting together is a culture of reckless love.

Be a community that demonstrates God's reckless love.

One Church That's UnLearning

Ecclesia, downtown Houston, Texas
www.ecclesiahouston.org

QUICK DESCRIPTION: A holistic, authentic Christian community that focuses on how God's narrative intersects the stories of our lives.

HISTORY: Several Baptist denominations; started in 1999.

ATTENDANCE: two hundred in one Sunday-evening worship service

THEME: Redeeming the Surrounding Culture

WHAT THE LEADER SAYS: "We are leaving behind the concepts of sacred and secular. We don't make a distinction between them. God is everywhere and has not been dismissed from the secular arena like most boomers think.

"Culture is to be met, embraced, and transformed. So we prefer to talk about what has been redeemed or in need of reception. We want to redeem culture, not remove ourselves from it. We don't focus much on developing programs for the church but on whether something is relational. We enter culture and engage people where they are."

—*Chris Seay, pastor, has been with the church since its beginning; age late twenties.*

How Are **you** UnLearning?

- What does your church need to unLearn in order to become a community that demonstrates God's reckless love?

- What color is God's love? What does it feel like?

- Draw something that represents a concrete demonstration of God's reckless love in your situation.

- What actions could you take to experience more of God's love?

ENDNOTES

1. Scott R. Burson and Jerry L. Walls, *C.S. Lewis & Francis Schaeffer* (Downers Grove, IL: InterVarsity Press, 1998), 29-30.

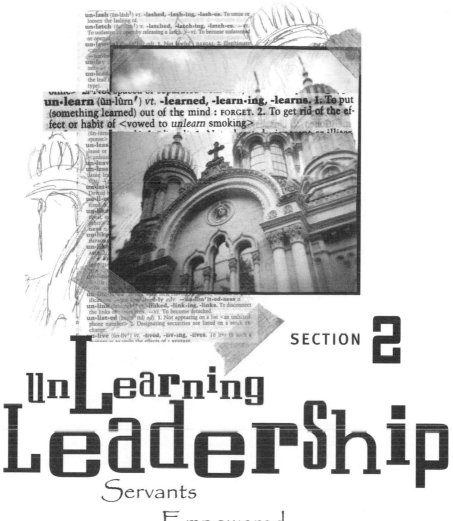

SECTION **2**

UnLearning
LeaderShip

Servants
Empowered
to Do
the Mission of Jesus

9

Replicating the DNA

Leaders are the carriers of the DNA, the shapers of the core values, the influencers. Churches become what their leaders embody. They replicate whatever the leader models.

In ancient Israel, Nicodemus was the premier example of religious correctness. He practiced all the rules and regulations. The crowds recognized him as a religious authority.

But when Nicodemus met with Jesus, he heard some news that was difficult to accept. Jesus told him that he needed to be "born from above" (John 3:3).

Jesus said that in order to "enter the kingdom of God" (John 3:5), your very being must be invaded by the Spirit of God. The Spirit's presence in people "born of the Spirit" (John 3:6) makes them like Jesus. We share Jesus' life force, his spiritual DNA.

When you immerse yourself in Jesus, you will do more than merely sample the Christian life. Immersion means taking on the nature, desires, passions, and behavior of Jesus. You share a God-life infinitely filled with joy, mercy, love, and hope. God creates new life through you.

I AM UNLEARNING THE IDEA THAT CHRISTIANITY IS ABOUT believing IN JESUS. IT'S REALLY ABOUT THE LIFE OF JESUS coming into your life AND MINE.

We begin to look and act like Jesus.

Spiritual leaders are the carriers of God's DNA in the church, the shapers of a church's vision and core values. They are the influencers of what the church embodies.

Christian leadership books today tend to deal with the ideology of leadership style, of embracing technology, or of innovative methodology. UnLearning leaders are going way beyond these emphases. They are more interested in the spirit, content, and soul of leadership. They focus their attention on those who serve as trainer-coaches.

AS PEOPLE PRESS TOWARD RADICAL DISCIPLESHIP, THEY REPLICATE THE DNA OF THE HOLY SPIRIT

throughout the church and community.

The key to radical discipleship is the development of trainer-coaches who carry the DNA to the edges of the movement.

DISCIPLESHIP REQUIRES MENTORING

The biblical model of discipleship is not directly based on an institutional teacher-classroom methodology.

DISCIPLESHIP EMERGES FROM

a mentoring model.

It happens between a leader-coach and an intimate group. The idea is outlined in Scripture as early as Exodus 18, when Moses' father-in-law told him that something was not working. "They're not changing, and it's wearing you out," Jethro explained in effect.

The apostles in the early church devoted themselves to prayer and the ministry of the Word. (See Acts 6:4.) They let others do everything else. Today the job of the chief spiritual leader remains the same: to lead the congregation in prayer and to teach the people the purposes and principles of God. Emerging churches have learned to partner with as many as several thousand coaches—leaders of ten—who focus on the personal development of each individual.

A teacher generally offers an overall prescription for the entire group. The trainer-coach applies biblical life principles to the unique needs of the individual.

In the larger classes I took at college, the professor was the master teacher, while the graduate assistant was the accessible mentor who knew my name. The assistants were there to demonstrate and explain what the professor talked about. They converted ideas into action. They gave specific-situation feedback.

At Ginghamsburg, we say that celebration—our corporate worship of God—is

important, but we also urge people to go to the next step. By becoming part of a cell—a small group or class—they get to know people who will become their trainer-coaches in day-to-day life. Trainer-coaches help us be faithful to our promises through demonstration, encouragement, and accountability.

When a pastor is unable, due to attendance growth, to give attention to everyone's personal development needs, then trainer-coaches are needed. (Generally that first happens at attendances of fifty and higher.) Trainer-coaches are at the heart of faith-building in the biblical plan. They help others achieve their God destiny.

Every other Thursday morning at 6:45, I meet with three men on our church board for the purpose of counsel. Together as leaders in this church, we hold each other accountable through the Word and prayer as we direct areas we're responsible for in the life of Ginghamsburg. This accountability group is essential to my spiritual well-being.

DEVELOPING LEADERS AS TRAINER-COACHES

I remember going to a movie with Carolyn and marveling at the physical fitness of lead actor Harrison Ford. "He's ten years older than I am, so how can his abs look so chiseled?" I asked her. She explained that he has a personal trainer. These coaches are knowledgeable in muscle development, diet, and human motivations. They know how to take ideas and turn them into realities in people's lives.

WHEN THE GROUP BECOMES TOO LARGE FOR PERSONALIZED TRAINING, YOU HAVE BECOME A teacher, NOT A MENTOR-COACH.

Through encouragement, demonstration, and faith a personal trainer promotes personal discipline for the purpose of achieving desired results. Spiritual leaders are in the business of faith development. Their purpose is to provoke personal discipline to achieve God's desired results. I'm a teacher to the overall church, but a personal trainer is someone able, as the name implies, to personalize training for each of the needs in an individual's life, often in the context of a group of about ten.

MY PRIMARY responsibility IN PASSING ON THE DNA OF THE SPIRIT TO THE PEOPLE OF GINGHAMSBURG CHURCH IS TO BE a teacher to trainer-coaches.

The key role in the life of the church is the leader of the group of ten.

The trainer-coach implements ideas and directions that come through the teaching pastors. These unpaid servants each take responsibility for a handful of individuals in the congregation, sometimes meeting with them in small cell groups and sometimes one-on-one. A well-developed network of trainer-coaches can implement ideas and teaching throughout the life of the entire congregation.

TRAINER-COACHES KNOW YOUR NAME

Erwin "Frosty" Brown is an American Legion baseball coach who has helped obtain some two hundred college scholarships for his players. Among those he has taken under his wing, ten young men have made it to the pros.

In our area of Ohio, anyone who wants to play college baseball works hard to make Frosty's Miami County team. Once players are on the team, Frosty becomes an integral part of their disciplined training, long before they play the first game of the season. He has a batting cage in his garage that "his boys" use throughout the year. His players can call him from anywhere and ask, "Coach, what's wrong with my swing?"

Frosty was my son Jonathan's summer coach for his final three years of high school. Many days I'd come home and see Jonathan talking with Frosty by phone, receiving personal tips about his hitting or fielding. When it was time for Jonathan to head out to college, Frosty wrote a note to thank Jonathan for three years on the team. The letter also encouraged Jonathan in his upcoming baseball years on an Ivy League University team. Frosty concluded his note by writing, "Never forget the old coach who believes in you."

Frosty demonstrates the DNA of the baseball world with a contagious passion and enthusiasm. And he continues to be a disciplined student of the game.

Who are the people in our churches who are equally effective at replicating the DNA of the Spirit of God?

UnLearning Moment

What is one recent relationship you can identify in which you were or are a mentor or disciple?

SERIOUS PREPARATION REQUIRED

The trainer-coach prepares seriously for the mentoring relationship. As our children were growing up, I coached baseball for nine years. It was a challenge to keep all fifteen players engaged. We never had a practice without an overall plan. We also had to formulate a different plan for each child. For one home-run hitter, our goal was to lay the foundation for a possible future as a college player. For another boy on the team, the most important thing we could teach him was how to wear a baseball cap right so the other kids wouldn't tease him.

I use the word *we* because I'd be crazy to try to be a trainer-coach to those fifteen boys alone. I had to do it with a leadership team. If I didn't have others who were making me sharper, my ideas would become stale.

AT CHURCH I AM UNLEARNING HOW TO BE A solo leader.

I develop my teachings as part of a team. We design each weekend worship experience with supplemental curriculum for the trainer-coaches to use. It's also used in various small groups and by individuals in their daily devotional readings.*

We help trainer-coaches break down the parts of the training experience. In Luke 9–10, Jesus taught his disciples and then sent them out in small teams to practice what he had shown them. Then they had a report-back time. That's our overall model.

We teach our trainer-coaches to regularly cover such areas of relationship-based discipleship as group-building skills, mentoring of others, prayer, service, financial stewardship, and witness. They take the people they're discipling through one or more of these elements, and then they give them the equivalent of homework.

"Will you grow?" is our constant emphasis. We know we're called to grow, but will we actually make the choice to grow?

BRUSH WITH DEATH JOLTS ME TOWARD ACTION

A surprise experience changed my life in a moment. It was August 18, 2000. Carolyn and I were sitting in a restaurant in Cincinnati with my sister and brother-in-law. I started to feel sick. I thought to myself, "Am I going to throw up? Or do I have to go to the bathroom? What's the matter with me?"

Carolyn noticed my fading color and said, "What's wrong?"

---

* See the appendix for Deeper Impact samples. They're also available on the church's Web site, www.ginghamsburg.org.

"I feel like I am going to faint." Then I collapsed into Carolyn's lap.

A doctor at the next table came over. Amazingly, I wasn't completely out. I could hear everything going on. I heard him say, "I can't get a pulse."

The emergency team was there in five minutes. The medics got me downstairs and into the ambulance. I heard one of them say, "His heart is arrhythmic, and his blood pressure is 60/40. Tell his family." They shoved aspirins into my mouth and asked me to chew them. The helplessness I felt was humbling.

During my trip to the emergency room, I was reminded that I am not in control. I lost any illusion that I can secure my future through hard work, accomplishments, or possessions. Without God's life I am nothing. Dust.

The opening pages of Genesis say that God created humanity from the dust of the earth. Dust is rather useless stuff. The difference occurred when God breathed the breath of life into the dust. The breath of God—wow!

This body of dust has now become the temple of God because the Holy Spirit lives in me. (See 1 Corinthians 3:16-17.) Can you believe it? God lives in me. I am a container of the divine!

My body is not my own. It is the temple of the Holy Spirit. My restaurant wake-up call signaled to me that if it's God's body, I had better get it into shape.

LIFE TRANSFORMATION CAN BE PAINFUL

Immediately after my heart scare, I went to see a cardiologist. He taught me about my body. He said I haven't taken the best care of it in recent years. But he wasn't the one who could help me on a day-by-day basis.

The recovery experience has caused me to shift my healthy lifestyle strategy from belief to faith.

I HAVE ALWAYS *believed* IN EXERCISE.

I AM NOW *acting* ON IT.

My body fat content was in the thirties—a ridiculously high level. So in October of 2000, I started working with a personal trainer. She is working with me to increase my heart strength.

When we're doing weights, she tells me I'm developing muscle mass and turning some of my fat into muscle. She reminds me, "Strength comes only through resistance." When I get to the place where I think I can't do any more, she says, "Five more lifts." She wants to push me through the threshold of my resistance.

Only as I push myself

PAST THE THRESHOLD OF "QUIT" WILL I DEVELOP

MORE HEALTH AND STRENGTH.

My trainer has worked with me to determine a pathway of desired results. I have found that to achieve those outcomes, I have to stretch continually to the next level. That means I have to keep pushing despite the pain. As soon as I could run 1.6 miles in twenty-five minutes, she turned up the pace.

When I gasp, "I've gone as far as I can go," she will say, "Two more minutes." And her two minutes aren't the same length as my two minutes!

In any athletic endeavor, there is no gain without pain. My trainer always says, "Do you feel the burn?" If I say "no," she changes the weight, and we do another set.

"Do you feel the burn now?" she asks. This time I say "yes."

"OK, let's change the weight again," she continues.

She's happy when I hurt. She says I'm never going to accomplish what I need to do if I don't feel the burn.

NO PAIN, NO GAIN

RESISTANCE DEVELOPS PERSEVERANCE.

Perseverance develops faith,

AND WITHOUT FAITH THE FULFILLMENT OF GOD'S PROMISE WILL NOT HAPPEN.

As a friend told me, "Take care of your body like you'll live forever and your soul like you'll die tomorrow."

It's working. I have more energy today than I had two years ago.

Experts say you're supposed to do twenty minutes of cardiovascular exercise at least four times a week. I'm trying to do something every day. It's painful, but I'm seeing results.

Why are so many of us not physically fit and lacking a committed physical regimen every week? Because it's hard! Why are most of us in church not spiritually fit or lacking in spiritual regimen? For the same reason: Sticking with it is hard.

If we are going to carry Christ everywhere we go, we have to do healthy things. It is going to be hard.

The difficult thing about exercise is that you have to keep doing it! I wish I could achieve the goal I want to attain and then not have to exercise any more.

That's what many people hope for, and I could easily become one of them. Unfortunately, as soon as we stop exercising, we begin to go backward.

MUCH OF THE NEW TESTAMENT IS A challenge TO PERSEVERANCE.

One example is Hebrews 10:23: "Let's keep a firm grip on the promises that keep us going" (*The Message*). Another translation calls us to "hold fast to the confession of our hope without wavering, for he who has promised is faithful" (NRSV). Another begins, "hold unswervingly" (NIV).

Paul likens our walk with Christ to athletic training. "Do you not know that in a race the runners all compete, but only one receives the prize? Run in such a way that you may win it. Athletes exercise self-control in all things; they do it to receive a perishable wreath, but we an imperishable one. So I do not run aimlessly, nor do I box as though beating the air; but I punish my body and enslave it, so that after proclaiming to others I myself should not be disqualified" (1 Corinthians 9:24-27).

Faith is hard work. One of the negatives of the modern church is that it has taught an easy believe-ism. We are saved by faith, not by belief. In the church today, many people think they're saved by right beliefs.

Faith is different from belief. I believe a lot of things that don't impact my day-to-day living. I believe in exercise. I have no doubt that people live longer and are healthier if they exercise. Many of us believe in exercise, but believing is not the same as doing.

I NEED A PERSONAL TRAINER TO TURN MY belief into faith.

THE HARD WORK OF FAITH

Faith is acting on the directive of God. It requires obedient action. Faith is successful only when action accompanies it.

The book of Acts records how God did an amazing work on the day of Pentecost through the entrance of the Holy Spirit. The power of God brought about drastic change in people's lives. They hung out with each other day in and out. They encouraged, cheered, and fanned into a flame the spark of the Spirit in each believer.

As the newness began to wear off, exuberant daily encounters turned into

weekly institutional meetings. At a later point, some communities of believers even gave up meeting altogether. The writer of Hebrews had to remind them: "Let's see how inventive we can be in encouraging love and helping out, not avoiding worshiping together as some do but spurring each other on" (Hebrews 10:24-25, *The Message*). The reference here to meeting together does not indicate only a weekly worship celebration. It means to live in a daily countercultural community as personal coaches to one another.

POWERING THE DNA

In ancient times, a fire carrier was the person responsible for moving the fire from one encampment to another as the tribe journeyed in its pursuit of food. This person often wore a specially made pouch that made it easier to transport a burning coal or ember.[1] For a nomadic tribe that depended on fire for cooking, warmth, or protection, the member who served as fire carrier bore a huge responsibility for the tribe's survival.

You are a fire carrier of a different sort. You carry the fire of God's Spirit to places dependent on that flame of God-life in you.

You are not the sole fire carrier, though. All who are faithful in Jesus have been "marked with the seal of the promised Holy Spirit" (Ephesians 1:13b). The fire of God is in them and goes wherever they go also.

The job of the leader is to take those fire carriers to the next place of God's leading. Our churches become what the leader embodies. They replicate the leader who shapes them.

One Church That's
UnLearning

Warehouse 242, downtown Charlotte, North Carolina
www.warehouse242.org

QUICK DESCRIPTION: A church connecting postmodern people to real relationships.
HISTORY: Evangelical Presbyterian Church; started in 1999.
ATTENDANCE: five hundred in one weekend service
THEME: No More Solo Leaders

WHAT THE LEADER SAYS: "I have had to unLearn that the vision for ministry comes primarily from the senior leader and is then disseminated down through the ranks. In fact, the vision is given to the people, and the job of the leader in partnership with the people is to discern, articulate, shape, and then champion the vision God has already given to the people he or she gets to lead.

"This means the first job of the leader is to listen—to God, to the people he or she is leading, and to the culture around. And at every point in the visioning process, the leader has to trust—God, certainly, but also the presence of the Holy Spirit in the life of the community. The Holy Spirit's work flows most freely when our leaders give up control and choose to trust, even in risky ways. The job of the leader is a vital one, but it is a secondary one. We don't come up with stuff on our own; rather, we work with the raw material God the Spirit has already placed in the hearts of the community we lead."

—*Todd Hahn, lead pastor, has been with the church since its beginning; age early thirties.*

How Are **you** UnLearning?

- Why are you making the changes you currently are introducing in the church you serve?

- To what extent do they implant the DNA of the movement into others?

- Write the prayer that flows from you as you read this chapter.

ENDNOTES

1. *Dictionary of Daily Life of Indians of the Americas, Vol. II* (Newport Beach, CA: American Indian Publishers, 1981), 739.

Living Hard

UnLearning leaders demonstrate the presence of the rule of God. God's people must demonstrate what relationships look like when Jesus Christ is Lord.

Jesus lived in an era when well-trained religious leaders were on every corner, yet people didn't seek them out. These leaders were neither relevant nor contagious.

The people were seeking the presence of God, not rules and judgmental corrections. Some even left the comforts of Jerusalem's gorgeous Temple with its splendidly attired priests and went out to the wilderness. They listened to a prophet named John who wasn't deemed religiously correct or within the boundaries of traditional expressions of faith.

John was different from the religious leaders of his day because of what his life displayed. John was someone who knew and experienced God in a way that seemed authentic. One biographer of John Wesley, the eighteenth-century evangelist and founder of Methodism, described him as "a flame going up and down the land, lighting candles such as, by God's grace, would never be put out."[1]

Catch on fire for God, and people will come to watch you burn.

UnLearning leaders know what it's like to feel the burn.

I am unLearning the idea that my primary objective as a leader is to grow, innovate, compete, or inform. Instead we are called first to demonstrate the presence of the rule of God.

SPIRITUAL LEADERS ARE A
visual demonstration OF GOD'S POWER.

A WATCH-ME DEMONSTRATION OF GOD'S POWER

Jesus spoke most about the kingdom of God. The Gospels contain more than one hundred references to God's kingdom. Jesus emphasized that the power of God's kingdom has come. Through Jesus, it was already present among his followers.

Jesus taught as one having authority, with power that fully demonstrated an attitude that might be summarized as, "Watch me and see that the presence of

God has appeared." The Bible says that "the crowds were astounded at his teaching" (Matthew 7:28b) because it was different from what the scribes modeled as they taught.

The world isn't interested in Christianity
BECAUSE WE CHRISTIANS AREN'T KNOWN AS PEOPLE
WHO LIVE WHAT WE SAY.

One of the fastest-growing religions in America is Buddhism because its followers tend to practice what they believe. I once heard MIT (Massachusetts Institute of Technology) scholar Peter Senge tell a Leadership Network gathering of pastors that an increasing number of Americans will be drawn to Buddhism because they perceive it as a more practical religion than Christianity.

Buddhism is centered in practice rather than doctrine. UnLearning leaders are returning to the ancient Christian emphasis of practice and faith-development rather than a narrow view of information transfer.

Christians try to reduce faith to easy believe-ism or social activism. Neither is fully what God has in mind. The former emphasizes a Monopoly-like card that reads, "You are authorized to pass Go and skip hell because you have made a mental decision." Too many Christians excuse their actions by posting bumper stickers that read, "Christians aren't perfect, just forgiven." They use it as a license to be as liberated from godly behavior as everyone else. They say, in effect, "Don't expect anything different from me."

I grew up in what might be called the First Church of the Frigidaire because the spiritual climate was so cold. I got connected with Jesus in my college years at the University of Cincinnati. I couldn't believe the change in my life. I figured most other serious followers of Jesus were as excited as I was.

Driving on the expressway, I saw my first "Honk if you love Jesus" bumper sticker. "Wow, there's another person who has been changed by Jesus," I said to myself. So I blew my horn. The driver ignored me, so I did a series of horn toots. Finally the guy looked at me and gave me a middle-finger gesture that he learned from someone other than Jesus!

KNOWN FOR A LIFESTYLE LIKE JESUS'

A Christian isn't someone who makes an intellectual statement of belief or who commits to a lifestyle of little do-good-isms that have no spiritual motivation.

A Christian is someone who is like Jesus.

In its earliest years, the word *Christian* was derogatory. It meant "Christs-people."[2] Roman soldiers would look at the "little Christs" and say, "This is amazing. We can spit in these people's faces, and they won't retaliate. They've taken on the lifestyle of Jesus."

Roman armies had an inexpensive way of outfitting their troops for the winter. They could stop anyone and say, "I'm a soldier; give me your coat." You had to do it. They had a similar way of moving equipment. A soldier could stop anyone and command, "Carry my pack." You had to carry it for a mile. At the end of the mile you could stop, set the pack down, and say, "I've done my duty according to Roman law." They'd grab another person.

"Not these Christians!" said the Romans. "When we take one of their coats, they voluntarily offer more: 'Would you like the shirt I bought to match it?' Or at the end of a mile, the Christian says, 'I'm ready to go a second mile.' "[3]

In the third century, I've heard, Christians were so persecuted that they'd be forced to walk naked on frozen ponds as incentive to give up their faith in a risen Lord. Entire families would go to their deaths singing songs to their God.

UnLearning Moment

What is one way you've led your congregation to go against popular or religious culture in a quest to demonstrate the lifestyle of Jesus?

What would happen today if we as leaders were more concerned with

integrity of lifestyle

than size of institution?

More than fifty years ago, A.W. Tozer warned that a whole new generation of Christians had grown up believing it is possible to follow Christ without forsaking the world.[4]

This watered-down form of cultural Christianity is alien to the emerging new breed of leader. Leaders in next-generation churches are learning how to minimize church meetings and to maximize life.

We have diluted the meaning of *Christian* in our culture today because we have verbalized faith without obedience. We have trivialized the meaning of *Christian*.

GOD'S PLAN TO CHANGE THE WORLD IS TO EQUIP PEOPLE TO LIVE
the way Jesus lived.

"Let your light shine before others, so that they may see your good works and give glory to your Father in heaven" (Matthew 5:16).

It has been said that the greatest distance in the universe is the gap between *knowing* what's right and *doing* what's right. I regularly speak at conferences, and I include a time for questions during or after my message. One question has stuck with me for a long time. I remember one pastor raising her hand and asking, "You have more than 3,000 people a week who attend Ginghamsburg and only 1,100 people who have made the commitment to membership. How many are really committed?"

She was thinking that I would respond with a figure of somewhere between 1,100 and 3,000. I stood there and thought for a moment. I estimated that in any given month, about seven to eight thousand different people show up on campus at one time or another. Of all those people, maybe about five hundred seem really committed. Perhaps five hundred people have acted on their decisions.

A lot of people have made decisions for Jesus. Very few have ever acted on those decisions. More than ever, leaders must model what life is like when Jesus is Lord.

WORKING FOR A FRIEND

It's easy to gloss over Jesus' statement, "No one has greater love than this, to lay down one's life for one's friends" (John 15:13). A serious read of what Jesus says next jolts anyone's understanding of a relationship with God: "I do not call you servants any longer...but I have called you friends, because I have made known to you everything that I have heard from my Father" (John 15:15).

JESUS CHRIST IS NOT PROMOTING
a religion.

He certainly wasn't intending to start a new religion. I don't see anywhere that he instructed people to go out and build institutions or even create names for ourselves, like Methodist, Baptist, Lutheran, True Church, United Church, Brethren in Christ, or Church of Christ.

JESUS IS OFFERING AN *intimate relationship* WITH GOD TO ALL PEOPLE ON PLANET EARTH.

Jesus says, "This is eternal life, that they may know you, the only true God, and Jesus Christ whom you have sent" (John 17:3).

Many people before Jesus' time thought God was a great, awesome, and powerful force—a manipulator, a giant cosmic being in the sky who toyed with people as a child would play with an anthill and a stick.

When they thought about relating to God, their relationship was always one of appeasement based upon fear. "How can I keep from ticking God off?" they would wonder. They came up with all kinds of superstitions that involved applying the right magical formula or knowing the right catchword. It was the equivalent of our modern-day sayings such as "never walk under a ladder" and "never let a black cat cross your path."

The emphasis was on what we could do to make God happy with us. People assumed that things would go badly if they didn't measure up.

FOR MANY OF THEM, THE WORD *God* didn't belong in the same sentence WITH THE WORDS *INTIMATE RELATIONSHIP*.

The same is true for many people today. Not too long after I began following Jesus, I married Carolyn, and we began our family. A few years later, when we put our firstborn on the school bus, I remember older, well-intentioned Christians asking us, "Did you plead the blood of Jesus over her?"

I didn't yet understand that God doesn't listen for key words and phrases in an attempt to hold back blessings. Instead, God's responses to us are based on our heart relationship. So I turned to my wife with fear and said, "Oh, Carolyn, I didn't pray the right words. Now the bus may have an accident."

FRIENDSHIP WITH GOD IS NOT BASED ON *my performance.*

How many times have you messed up, gone to your prayer room or church, and pleaded to God, "Just give me one more chance." Those words suggest a friendship based on performance, and that's not what our relationship with God is about. Jesus says that he has revealed everything to us; he has been vulnerable to us. Jesus is a true friend. God treats me as a best friend.

When I have a best friend, fear is absent from that relationship. There is nothing to fear, even when I mess up.

I was sitting next to a man at a baseball game not too long ago, and he said to me, "I have not been to church for over three years. When my dad went through cancer and all the suffering three years ago, I said, 'God, how could you do that to my dad?' "

Do we think that way sometimes? Do we assume that when something bad happens, God is behind it? I hate it when someone tells a child whose parent has died, "God needed your mother more than you did." No! A friend does not make bad things happen. "No one, when tempted, should say, 'I am being tempted by God'; for God cannot be tempted by evil and he himself tempts no one" (James 1:13).

Look at Jesus' reaction at the funeral of Lazarus. He wept. (See John 11:1-44.) Our God grieves when bad things happen. In death, God causes resurrection. God doesn't cause evil.

God redeems bad things

BECAUSE OF LOVE.

NO MORE SHAME

When God's people demonstrate relationships with Jesus as Lord, shame also disappears.

We all know our deficiencies, don't we? At times I can be so unlike Jesus that I feel horribly ashamed afterward. I have an anger-rage button. It doesn't get pressed too often, but every once in a while, I can be absolutely mean. I'm also tempted for the private Mike Slaughter to be different from the public Mike Slaughter, and sometimes I give in. You can't believe some of the ugly thoughts and temptations that come to my mind. They come to all of us.

When these things happen, we think to ourselves that God must be less than pleased with us. So we become lost in life's distractions and interruptions. We keep a distance from God because we think hiding might help.

In Genesis, after Adam and Eve had sinned, God asked them why they were hiding. That was a powerful question.

Adam responded, "I heard the sound of you in the garden, and I was afraid, because I was naked; and I hid myself" (Genesis 3:10). The issue of shame, for most of us, remains hidden deep and unresolved. We cover ourselves and hide behind meaningless clutter. We fill ourselves with busyness. Our lives run into endless lines of guarded, unfocused activity.

It doesn't have to be that way. God's Spirit can invade our very being, removing our shame and changing us into the Christ-bearers that we were created to be. Jesus did not come to judge the world, "but in order that the world might be saved through him" (John 3:17).

IF GOD does not condemn us

AND IS NOT WILLING THAT ANY SHOULD PERISH,

THEN WE CAN WALK without fear,

RISKING AND GIVING OURSELVES HONESTLY TO OTHERS.

The power of leadership occurs as people touch other people's shame and pain through a demonstration of authentic relationships.

DEMONSTRATING A GOD-CENTERED RELATIONSHIP

Eight hundred years before Christ was born, the prophet Isaiah wrote the prophecy sung in Handel's *Messiah* and quoted in many Christmas cards: "A virgin shall conceive, and bear a son, and shall call his name Immanuel" (Isaiah 7:14b, KJV). *Immanuel* means "God is with us."

The miracle of Christmas is that God was born in human form.

THE MIRACLE OF THE CHRISTIAN LIFE IS THAT

God is born *in* us.

Christianity is not fundamentally a belief system. It is not an academic discussion to be defended.

God has supernaturally entered the life of all who give themselves to Jesus Christ, and that life begins to grow in us. As Jesus lives through us, we are God-bearers. We are marked by the life of God. We carry the light of Christ. The church is most effective when leaders demonstrate Christ's light and life to each other.

One Church That's
UnLearning

Solomon's Porch, urban neighborhood of Minneapolis, Minnesota. www.SolomonsPorch.com

QUICK DESCRIPTION: Solomon's Porch is not a "religious service provider" but rather a gathering of people who are on a pilgrimage through life with each other and with God. Our gatherings for worship are designed to help us all along on that journey.

HISTORY: affiliated with the Evangelical Covenant Church; started in 2000.

ATTENDANCE: two hundred in two Sunday-evening services

THEME: Holistic, Missional Christian Community

WHAT THE LEADER SAYS: "We are unLearning what it means to be Christian. For many of us, Christianity has been based around individualism and a strong Bible focus. We are in the process of experiencing faith through a mode of collective interactions. The idea is to bring people into Christian community (local, global, and historical) and allow that community to reshape our lives and reorder our way of being. We have moved away from using education (Sunday school or other teaching modes) or even a relational model (small groups and the like) and are attempting to use a community approach. This has impacted the way we pray, preach, sing, trust, share, and exchange life.

"We are also in the process of using hospitality as the primary connecting point and preaching as secondary. This has affected the way our space looks (couches and chairs instead of a stage), how we speak (from all around the space and not just the front), the role of the sermon, and the way we do Holy Communion (as a weekly house 'party')."

—*Doug Pagitt, pastor, has been with the church since its beginning; age early thirties.*

- What has God been teaching you about how you relate to others? What have you been unLearning about what relationships look like when Jesus Christ is Lord?

- How are you training others to grow in that kind of relationship?

- What do you want to say to God in light of this chapter? to yourself?

ENDNOTES

1. *The Master Christian Library, vol. 1-4, Sage Digital Library*, "John Wesley" (Sage Software, 1995).
2. F.F. Bruce, *Commentary on the Book of the Acts* (Grand Rapids, MI: Wm. B. Eerdmans Publishing Co, 1977), 241.
3. Robert Smith, *Augsberg Commentary on the New Testament: Matthew* (Minneapolis, MN: Augsburg Publishing House), 103.
4. Ron Eggert, Tozer Topical Reader, Vol. II (Camp Hill, PA: Christian Publications, 1998), 276-277.

The Smell of God

Leaders influence people most through integrity of heart. Spiritual influence goes beyond methodologies to the passion of the Spirit. UnLearning leaders begin to smell like God.

Jesus was an influencer. He came into the world to be a source of redemption. His mission would glorify God, benefit others, and bring joy to himself.

Would there have been anything wrong with Jesus using his power to turn stones into bread when he was famished? Or with forcing the kind of context in which angels would need to pamper him after his forty-day fast in the rugged wilderness? After all, he was the Son of God.

Those are the angles Satan used to tempt Jesus. Satan's temptation offered Jesus the alternatives of personal gratification, success, status, and recognition. (See Matthew 4:1-11; Luke 4:1-13.)

The change would have been ever so subtle at first. Then an alternative, fatal pathway would have emerged. If Jesus had said "yes," demonic influences would have attached themselves to the authentic call of God in his life, manipulating it and distorting it. Jesus would have shifted from being God-centered, where his whole purpose was to glorify and honor God, to an ego-centered mission.

I recently learned that one of the Doctor of Ministry students I worked with had an extramarital affair. He was starting a new church, and he did a crash and burn. Too often the reason for failure is that people begin to see themselves as exceptions.

I AM unLearning
THE CEO LEADERSHIP MODEL THAT SURROUNDS ITSELF WITH AN ATTITUDE OF entitlement.

The danger of the CEO outlook is the expectation of a comfortable lifestyle. No longer do you become incarnate to the life of your people; you're the top of the organization, and you no longer identify with the life of people. Like little children, we can become enamored with our toys.

I am unLearning a mentality of consumer self-actualization. It permeates

American culture, and the church of Jesus Christ has been deeply infected by it.

OUR CONSUMER MENTALITY IS THE antithesis OF THE KINGDOM OF GOD.

God's call is to change to a servant mentality. The spiritual leader identifies with the suffering servant.

PASSION FROM THE HEART

What does it mean to be identified with the suffering servant? David—in his former, better days—is the example used in Psalm 78:70-72 to offer a biblical model for leadership. These verses give us two critical leadership traits: integrity of heart and skillful hands. These ideas, if applied, are enough to spark a revolutionary movement.

First and foremost, David was a Spirit-anointed leader. It is through our spirit that we influence people the most. Psalm 78:70 says God "chose his servant David, and took him from the sheepfolds." God interwove David's boyhood life experience and skills with a greater spiritual purpose.

When the prophet Samuel looked for the person to anoint as the next king, God rebuked him for looking primarily at the outward appearance. True, David was not a logical choice. David had brothers, all of them older and apparently bigger, stronger, better looking, smarter, and more experienced. David was just a child. Why did God choose David?

God passed over David's more handsome, older brothers and chose David to succeed Saul and become king of Israel. As the Lord explained to Samuel, concerning one of David's older brothers, "Do not look on his appearance or on the height of his stature, because I have rejected him; for the Lord does not see as mortals see; they look on the outward appearance, but the Lord looks on the heart" (1 Samuel 16:7).

Instead God selected David, not because of David's intellectual belief, but based on his heart. David had a passionate faith.

FAITH IS YOUR life passion, YOUR HEART FOCUS.

David had an incredible affair of the heart with God. What did his predecessor have? Saul had religion. Saul believed in God. Religion has to do with what you believe, what makes sense. Passion often goes beyond sense-making.

What happens when you have belief but you don't have a passionate affair of the heart? You live carefully, cautiously, and calculatingly. You can believe, believe, believe, but your life actions are going to be determined by your passion.

Belief will always give way to the presiding passion of your life. Jesus doesn't ask, "Do you believe in me?" His question is "Do you love me more than these?" (John 21:15b). Those who have victory over the temptations and struggles of life are those whose ultimate passion is the presence and call of Jesus Christ.

Jesus told his disciples, "I have said these things to you so that my joy may be in you, and that your joy may be complete" (John 15:11). Religion doesn't have anything to do with joy. Passion has everything to do with it.

UNLEARNING LEADERS EXUDE FROM THEIR PORES
passion for the kingdom
OF GOD.

Many of us have had a conversion of the head. We believe certain things are true. We accept as fact that Jesus is the Son of God, the Messiah, Savior of the world. I *believe* that Jesus was resurrected from the grave. I believe the body and Spirit of Jesus Christ came back to life. I believe he died for the forgiveness of my sins.

Some have gone from the conversion of the *head*—what we believe—to conversion of the *hands*. Believing certain truths, we go beyond belief to committing our lives to serving Jesus' purpose in the world. Many are tirelessly serving and committing themselves to a kingdom-honoring lifestyle.

Jesus is calling us to a conversion of the *heart*. He wants to be the all-consuming passion of your life. Passion is a desire that goes beyond reason.

Tom Lipps is on Ginghamsburg's worship team as our assistant director of music. He's a graduate of the University of Dayton with a degree in music. Tom says that when he's teaching kids to play the piano, they often want to be careful and cautious. They want to be technically correct with the music and hit all the right notes. Tom tells his students to practice a lot and to be precise, but not worry so much about making mistakes. It's more important to play with passion.

Life doesn't flow with technical precision. That's the problem in faith. With God, the Creator of the universe, we tend to hear the same message as those children at the piano. "Don't make any mistakes," we think God is saying. We want to do everything right and the way it's supposed to be done. But it's more important that we live our faith with passion.

In the movie *Mr. Holland's Opus*, Glenn Holland plays a recording of "Louie, Louie" for a struggling student. It has only three chords, but it was a hit because

the composer played it in such a way as to evoke passion.

Jesus Christ isn't calling us to focus on technical perfection in how we express our love for God.

JESUS IS CALLING US TO A PASSIONATE, ALL-CONSUMING, reckless love.

People are dying without Jesus. They're lonely and lost. They're in great pain from addictions. We need to run to the challenge of the battle. Passion is not careful, cautious, or calculated.

I am a baseball fan and a former little league coach. I have seen too many kids who get up to bat and don't want to strike out. On strike three, they are still standing there with their bats on their shoulders because they are afraid of striking out.

The same thing happens with followers of Jesus. Week after week I see too many people take out their wallets and give a token nod to God instead of an expression of everything they have. People don't take spiritual risks or do anything unless it makes total sense. Veteran Christians, including leaders, take on attitudes of entitlement. This behavior is a far cry from someone motivated by a passionate affair of the heart.

"By faith Abraham obeyed when he was called to set out for a place that he was to receive as an inheritance; and he set out, not knowing where he was going" (Hebrews 11:8). We Americans like the ready-aim-fire sequence. It's orderly and makes sense.

When was the last time you set out with your church on faith, not certain where you were going or what would be ahead? When God says, "Go!" what do you do? You go. All you know is that the voice within you, this passionate call of heart, is prompting you to go. It doesn't make sense, but you know God will provide and be there with you every step of the way.

UnLearning Moment

What is one recent way you've done just that—led your congregation forward on faith-driven passion, even though the facts didn't make sense?

TEMPTATION WITH ENTITLEMENT

King David had a God-given passion for significance. He led the nation of Israel into a golden age of enlarged borders, power, and influence. In situation after situation he followed God's leading. God even affirmed David as "a man after his own heart" (1 Samuel 13:14b).

David's temptation, just as subtle as what came to Jesus, was one of entitlement. Didn't he deserve to stay at home once in a while? Hadn't he trained enough soldiers to fight in his place? Wasn't living comfortably an appropriate next phase in his life as a leader?

David felt he was so privileged that he didn't need to go to battle. He delegated that task, and his decision compromised his spirit. He forgot that first and foremost, he was the spiritual leader to the people.

Then he got into big trouble. "In the spring of the year, the time when kings go out to battle...David remained at Jerusalem" (2 Samuel 11:1). He saw a beautiful woman named Bathsheba. "So David sent messengers to get her, and she came to him, and he lay with her" (2 Samuel 11:4a). In a later abuse of power, David arranged for Bathsheba's husband to be murdered. (See 2 Samuel 11:14-25.)

David was not alone in his sin. His predecessor, Saul, also saw himself as an exception, a person of special privilege. Both lost their role of spiritual leader as a result.

We're all going to make mistakes, but the Word says, "We know that all things work together for good for those who love God, who are called according to his purpose" (Romans 8:28). God's good work is not based on my successes or my failures. God's grace is not contingent on my goodness or badness, rightness or wrongness. Forgiveness is available because of Jesus' death and resurrection. None of us are righteous. Only Jesus is worthy.

A FOLLOWER OF JESUS HAS BEEN

invaded by Jesus' presence.

We have the ability to think God's thoughts. We can demonstrate God's actions. We literally take on the integrity of Jesus Christ. When I give myself fully to the promise of God's presence, the Spirit of Jesus rules in my life. My walk isn't based on my desires and my feelings but on God's good work within me.

David, in his better times, led "with upright heart" (Psalm 78:72a). David lived out of integrity of spirit. David was the kind of person God wants as a leader.

Think about the woman who came to Jesus "with an alabaster jar of very costly

ointment, and she poured it on his head as he sat at the table" (Matthew 26:7). The cost for this one bottle of perfume was more than a year's wages. (See Mark 14:5.) Jesus' followers got upset, saying the equivalent of "This is wasteful and irresponsible! Do you know how many poor folks that could have taken care of?" Quite possibly this woman was so beside herself in her passion for Jesus that she spent her dowry to purchase the ointment, which could mean no marriage and no children for her. She might have risked her entire future for Jesus.

The woman's action erupted out of unchecked emotion. It was an irrational act of unreasonable passion. Yet it was also the kind of response that pleased Jesus.

Her action represents the next level to which God wants people to go. Too often we serve people's needs out of duty or obligation. God wants us to give the best we have, and to give it from the heart.

When we act out of conviction of heart, God combines our failures and victories together, and they become the will of God. You and I don't have to fear making mistakes. We simply live with passion out of the call of Jesus Christ upon us.

Integrity of heart is the first part of spiritual leadership.

USING YOUR GIFTS TO GUIDE OTHERS

Psalm 78 also notes that David was to lead with skillful hands. "David shepherded them with integrity of heart; with skillful hands he led them" (Psalm 78:72, NIV). David was a shepherd. God took note of David's unique gift mix and passion.

GOD USED DAVID'S "DAY JOB" SKILLS FOR A

kingdom purpose.

Most of us are Christians because of the fruit of other people's labor—faithful servants of God who gave their life for Jesus Christ and used their skills for the advancement of the kingdom.

One of the reasons I'm in ministry today is because of Mrs. Cook, a lady in the church where I grew up. On the way home from junior high, I'd regularly stop at her house for cookies. She'd tell me, "Mike, God has his hand on you in a powerful way. It's going to be amazing what God does when he harnesses all that energy in you." She took a group of junior and senior high students to a Methodist seminary near Columbus, Ohio, and she began to paint pictures of God-possibilities in our heads.

I struggled in school with less than average grades. Dale Renner was my sixth-grade public school teacher. He made me stay in at lunch after I had flunked one of his tests. He gave me half of his sandwich and then showed me the correct way to do the math problem. He gave me the test over again and then tore up the old one. He said, "It's not my job to average your failure. It's my job to teach you success." He'd also tell me about Jesus and how Jesus changed his life. Mr. Renner would come to my house and tutor me. He never charged my parents. He wouldn't allow me to fail. He felt this mission was his call from God.

I have a friend named Bill Young. He is a guide in Yellowstone Park. We went to graduate school together. The book *A Day in the Life of America* has a silhouette of Bill Young on the front cover.

When I was in Yellowstone one afternoon, Bill saddled up two horses and said, "Mike, we're going to ride eleven miles out Black Canyon." At certain places, we rode thirty feet above a river on ledges that were two or three feet wide. No guardrails or fences would protect us from a thirty-foot plunge if we stumbled or fell.

Why would I take this risk? I did it because I trusted Bill. He does it all the time. He is a guide. He is not a travel agent who sends people brochures with information. That's what many of us in the church have been. We have been travel agents who can provide information. Very few of us have been guides.

A guide is SOMEONE WHO CAN TRULY SAY, "BEEN THERE, DONE THAT, *AND STILL DOING IT.*"

A guide is like a trainer-coach.

In the Bible the phrase *to know* means to have a personal encounter with someone.[1] If I know Bill Young, I've done more than study his picture on the cover of *A Day in the Life of America*. In my spiritual journey, if I know God, I've done more than learn information from the Bible. It means I've met God in a personal way.

Paul prayed that the church would be "rooted and grounded in love" (Ephesians 3:17b). As Paul's prayer unfolds, it indicates that the love of Christ is more important than information—it "surpasses knowledge" (Ephesians 3:19a). Paul wanted the church to demonstrate the life of Christ in everyday, ordinary encounters. Above anything else, the Ephesian Christians were to know and demonstrate the revolutionary love of Christ. The reason was so that they "may be filled with all the fullness of God" (Ephesians 3:19b).

CARRYING THE SCENT OF GOD

We lead with integrity of heart, and we influence people most with our spirit.

Spirit influence

DOES MORE THAN OUR WISDOM, KNOWLEDGE, ELECTRONIC MEDIA,

AND ALL OF OUR METHODOLOGIES COMBINED.

People can smell the passion of the Spirit.

What does it smell like when God is present? Perhaps a fragrant incense? Or an aroma of a sweet perfume?

When God entered planet Earth as a human, the surrounding odors were unpleasant at best. Mary did not give birth in a place that smelled like cinnamon potpourri. She bore Jesus in a stall that reeked of cow dung, urine, hay, and donkey breath.

The suffering servant must identify with the worst conditions of humanity. I'll bet the Good Samaritan in Jesus' parable (Luke 10:33-37) didn't have rubber gloves. He didn't have time to protect himself. He risked getting the first-century equivalent of AIDS. He saw a person in need and used his own resources. Oil and wine were expensive items, but they smelled great! The Samaritan put the hurt man on his donkey—his own SUV—risking bloodstains on the leather seats.

Why treat others with sacred worth? Why share the scent of God? Because people are the objects of God's affection. It's a passion so strong that God pursues us to the point of death on a cross.

Sometimes God's smell is very sweet on us. The Apostle Paul described real followers of Jesus as those who smell like burning incense. "Because of Christ, we give off a sweet scent...Everywhere we go, people breathe in the exquisite fragrance" (2 Corinthians 2:15a, 14b, *The Message*).

Authenticity is having the scent of the Creator of the universe all over you.

THE behavior of Christ

DEMONSTRATED TO PRE-CHRISTIAN PEOPLE IS FAR MORE CONVINCING

THAN ALL OUR INTELLECTUAL EXPLANATION.

Leaders influence people most through integrity of heart. UnLearning leaders carry the scent of God.

One Church That's
UnLearning

Mission Hills Church, Littleton, Colorado
www.missionhills.org

QUICK DESCRIPTION: Bringing a generation to a relationship in Jesus Christ that surpasses all extremes, through genuine community, Bible-based teaching, authentic outreach, and passionate worship.

HISTORY: Baptist General Conference; Mission Hills Church started in 1949; The Edge started in 1998.

ATTENDANCE: seventy in one Sunday-evening service

THEME: Passion Over Methodology

WHAT THE LEADER SAYS: "At The Edge, a worship and teaching ministry designed to reach the twenty-something generation, we've had to unlearn the idea that everything has to be polished and produced. Postmoderns do not trust things that are slick. They want authenticity above other values. For postmoderns, process is as important as product, if not more so. We are always struggling to meet people where they are and help them go with Jesus to where they need to be without seeming contrived."

—Doug Zerbst, pastor of adult ministries, at the church since 1994; age mid-thirties.

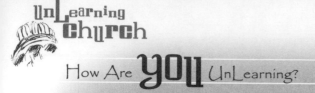
- Have you known a leader who "smells like God"? What scent did that person give off?

- Draw a picture to show what God smells like in your own life.

- What attitudes can you express or actions can you take to help you smell like God?

ENDNOTES

1. *The New International Dictionary of New Testament Theology*, vol. 2 (Grand Rapids, MI: The Zondervan Corporation, 1986), 392.

Working Your Sweet Spot

UnLearning leaders understand their God-wiring. They work out of their sweet spot, the center of their passion and giftedness. As they serve out of their personal call and gift mix, they honor God, benefit others, and experience personal joy.

Three of Jesus' disciples had a highly personal encounter with him in a place known as the Mount of Transfiguration. They were changed as a result.

As Jesus was praying on the mountain, "the appearance of his face changed, and his clothes became dazzling white. Suddenly they saw two men, Moses and Elijah, talking to him. They appeared in glory" (Luke 9:29-31a). Then something even more amazing happened: "A cloud came and overshadowed them; and they were terrified as they entered the cloud. Then from the cloud came a voice that said, 'This is my Son, my Chosen; listen to him!'" (Luke 9:34-35)

The very next day, a great crowd met them as they came down from the mountain. A man from the throng shouted, "Teacher, I beg you to look at my son; he is my only child. Suddenly a spirit seizes him, and all at once he shrieks. It convulses him until he foams at the mouth; it mauls him and will scarcely leave him. I begged your disciples to cast it out, but they could not" (Luke 9:38-40).

These were the disciples that yesterday had felt like they could do anything. "But today," each of them feels, "I can't do squat!"

You've been there, haven't you? Many of us call ourselves disciples of Jesus, and we are. Yesterday we had a glimpse of God, yet today we seem powerless. We are depleted, and we have nothing to give. We feel overwhelmed by demands, expectations, and lengthy to-do lists.

Everyone in America understands the expression "bad-hair day." We all have had bad-hair days. If we become really honest, there are times when we have spiritual and emotional "bad-hair" seasons.

We have also been on the mountain. We have had a glimpse of God. We feel we have touched the mystery. The cloud, that mystery of God, seemed so real.

Then the next day we come down and confront the pressures, demands, and expectations of life and ministry.

AT THAT POINT WE ASK,

"Where is God today?

I HAD A SPIRITUAL HIGH YESTERDAY, BUT WHERE IS GOD NOW?"

The life of following Jesus cannot be reduced to following five sequential steps or filling in the blanks. The reality of the Christian life is that you're up on the mountain one day, and you're deep in the valley the next. Following Jesus involves both escape and engagement. It's solitude and service. It's receiving and giving. It's full of things that don't seem to go together naturally.

ENERGIZED BY GOD'S PRESENCE

When you hit a tennis ball at the sweet spot of the racket, the ball takes off with seemingly little effort. The ball, almost on its own, just glides over the net.

When you're working outside of that center area, you can still hit it over the net, but it's a lot harder. That awkward vibrating feeling means you didn't connect in the sweet spot.

We have a deep need to connect to God and be effective in serving God's purpose. This need can lead us to an energy that can be described as working out of your sweet spot. When you live from your sweet spot, you will be connected to God, and you will maximize your personal potential for God's mission.

I AM UNLEARNING THE HABITS THAT KEEP ME FROM

focusing on my sweet spot—

THE CENTER OF MY PASSION AND GIFTEDNESS—

AND THE INTIMACY WITH GOD AND THE FRUITFULNESS IT LEADS TO.

My son often comes up to me after a baseball game, and I'll tell him what a great hit he had. He'll respond, "Dad, I just missed it." I know exactly what he means. He hit the ball a little bit down on the handle or a little too close to the end. Otherwise it would have gone out of the ballpark.

Next-wave leaders know where their sweet spot is, and they work out of that fine-tuned place of effectiveness. They know how they have been God-wired. God has made you for the specific purpose of connecting to your God destiny.

WHEN YOU ARE LIVING
according to God's call IN YOUR LIFE,
YOU'RE LIVING OUT OF THE SWEET SPOT.

When you operate out of your call, you love what you do. The exercise gives you energy.

People ask how I can speak around the U.S. and Canada and then come back and speak at up to five worship celebrations in a weekend at Ginghamsburg. The reason is my "love to"—my sweet spot. I may be physically tired, but my whole being is energized by the presence of God.

Of all the places I go and all the things I get to do, I am never more in the sweet spot of God's created purpose for my life than when I am at Ginghamsburg, sharing the marvelous love of God in Jesus Christ with the congregation. This is where my heart sings the most. This is what I like to do the best.

In sports, there is a world of difference in life between a "can do" shot and a "love to" shot. The same is true with ministry that I *love* to do, compared to those activities I do merely because I *can*.

For me, counseling comes from "can do" abilities. When I used to do counseling in ministry, I'd draw on learning from my college degree in social work. I made myself spend an hour in preparation beforehand and then do twenty minutes of write-ups afterward. I can do counseling, but only with great energy drain.

I no longer do counseling ministry at Ginghamsburg. We found gifted lay people in the church, unpaid servants at first, whose "love to" was to do pastoral ministry. Since then the church's crisis care ministry has moved forward dramatically. Its counseling center has also blossomed with paid professionals partnering with unpaid lay persons doing pastoral care.

The apostles understood their sweet spot and said, in effect, "We cannot neglect the Word of God and prayer." They found people hard-wired by the Spirit who capably did food distribution for the widows. God received honor, the whole community of faith benefited, and those leaders who operated out of their sweet spot experienced joy. (See Acts 6:1-6.)

Good things happened as a result. "The word of God continued to spread; the number of the disciples increased greatly in Jerusalem, and a great many of the priests became obedient to the faith" (Acts 6:7).

What is the center of your passion and giftedness? You need to be able to put your finger on it.

EVERYTHING YOU TOUCH MULTIPLIES

LEADERS CAN'T LIVE out of the "can do" LONG-TERM AND BE HEALTHY AT THE SAME TIME.

Sometimes we can't avoid doing "can do" activities, but the wise leader will be strategizing how to move to the "love to."

How can you discern whether you're living out of "love to"? If you're living out of your sweet spot, you can't help but honor and glorify God. It will benefit and bless other people. It will bring you joy. Everything you touch will be multiplied for the kingdom of God.

Ask those who know you well—work colleagues, people you're mentoring, and your husband or wife. Ask them to describe what you seem to be *most* motivated to do (your heart passion) and where you are *most* fruitful (your effectiveness).

If you really want to be gutsy, ask your children what your ultimate passion is. They can identify it in a moment. They can tell if your passion is your work, your hobby, your lifestyle, or even if it is God. We don't fool anybody long-term.

As we grow older, we have a tendency to decelerate in our life dreams. Sometimes self-doubt hits us. Physical energy and stamina come into play. Years of coming against negative and resistant people began to take their toll. We begin to wonder if we still have what it takes. Enthusiasm and positive thinking will carry a person only so far.

Instead of being a source of healing and life to other people, we can become a source of irritation, confusion, and conflict. Once a young dreamer, too soon an aging cynic.

If you're spending more than 30 percent of your time in the "can do" realm, rather than the "love to" realm, you would be wise to come up with a plan for change.

THE POWER OF SIN

SIN IS A *gravity* THAT CAUSES US TO UNDERESTIMATE OUR *created purpose*, OUR OWN PERSONAL DESTINY.

We begin a trade-off and produce a life that is successful but not satisfying. We trade our spiritual destinies for a spirit of materialism. These are totally different spirits.

Then we become confused because sin is acting as a gravity. We have a sweet-spot passion that is meant for God's purpose, but we don't know what to do with it. In our confusion we transfer our passion. We bring other things into our personal space. We pour our passion into family, our jobs, growing our church, or our hobbies, all to the neglect of God. We produce a life that is successful but not satisfying.

As a result we underestimate the purpose for which God sent us.

When we allow Jesus to invade our personal space, the Holy Spirit allows us to de-gravitize. According to Ephesians, God is constantly poised "to accomplish abundantly far more than all we can ask or imagine" (3:20b) according to the Spirit working in us.

When I am not working from my sweet spot, I will be more prone to anger, quarrels, dissension, strife, idolatry, lust, and jealousy. Sin is the elevation of self-importance. It neglects my receptivity for God to re-create my heart. How many times have I acted out of anger and done what I know is wrong, and continued to do it, even when I know it is wrong?

Perhaps you are in leadership out of selfish ambition. You'll find it hard to identify your sweet spot.

Ego-centered people see everything through themselves. They always ask how something will affect them. "Will it benefit me or will it inconvenience me?"

Ego-centered people are the dominant figures in their world. Ego-centered Christians become bullies. When we are surrendered to the Spirit of God, we are people who demonstrate to the world the militant, radical love of Jesus Christ. But when we become an ego-centered people, we become judgmental, and we become mean. We may even begin saying, "God told me."

We become (we think) the voice of God. We no longer live out of our sweet spot. We play a role. Instead of living authentically, we perform an act.

TIME TO CLIMB THE MOUNTAIN

If that's where you are, why not make a change? To live in a way that will honor and glorify God, you have to lose yourself.

YOU HAVE TO GIVE UP

everything

TO FOLLOW JESUS.

As he said, "If any want to become my followers, let them deny themselves and take up their cross and follow me. For those who want to save their life will lose it, and those who lose their life for my sake will find it" (Matthew 16:24-25).

Here's one way you could make the change: "God, I ask you today for a holy restlessness, a hunger that will cause me to move toward that wonderful place of significance where I live out of the sweet spot of your created purpose for my life. I pray in Jesus' name, realizing my needs, my imperfections, my failures, my deceits, and my distractions. I also realize that I am your child, and you will never let me go. I stand before you. Strip me of my lies, my deceits, my lack of forgiveness, my pride, and my denial. Strip me that Jesus will live through me. Amen."

Allow Jesus to invade that personal space in your life where the Spirit connects you to your personal potential.

YOU WERE MADE TO BE

passionate

FOR GOD.

Don't spend your life on something so small that you accomplish it out of your "can do"—and that you do it without God.

God wants to be involved in the intimate, minute details of your life. Let God work through your sweet spot to create your future and to serve the kingdom.

One Church That's UnLearning

Rock Harbor, Costa Mesa, California
www.RockHarbor.org

QUICK DESCRIPTION: A place to belong, reach, grow, serve, and celebrate.

HISTORY: Nondenominational; affiliated with Mariners Church, Irvine, California; started in 1997.

ATTENDANCE: 1800 in two Sunday-morning services and two Sunday-evening services

THEME: Helping Others Find Their Sweet Spot of Giftedness

WHAT THE LEADER SAYS: "One of our most distinctive local expressions is the sense of teamwork that allows every person at Rock Harbor to serve in an area of giftedness and be the minister God shaped him or her to be. This means the primary role of staff is to equip volunteer leaders (we call them shepherds) who lead and serve entire teams of servers/ministers to use their gifts to build up the Body of Christ.

"To build that kind of identity, we've had to unLearn much about doing church. As Cindy Massaro, one of our lead team members, says, 'We've unLearned that the up-front teaching pastor is the "minister" expected to meet everyone's needs. We are all ministers working together as the body. The up-front teaching pastor is only using his gifts in that capacity.' Troy Murphy, another lead team member adds, 'Our most distinctive local expression comes through empowering our people to do the ministry. They are the priests of Rock Harbor.' Finally, Stacy Scott, another lead team member, offers an example: 'In each ministry role I have held, I have not had the experience in it to be able to do the work. I have had to seek out people from our church body to help make the ministry happen.' "

—*Keith Page, founding pastor of Rock Harbor in 1997; age mid-thirties.*

- What responsibilities do you need to turn away from to live out of your sweet spot? You may not yet know *how* these responsibilities can be carried by others. The starting point is to specifically identify the primary ones that represent your "can do" rather than your "love to."

- How can you lead others to discover and focus on their sweet spots, to live out of their call, passion, and giftedness?

- What is the shape and texture of your sweet spot?

- How does the message of this chapter challenge or comfort you?

Moving Together

Rather than manage the present, unLearning leaders paint
a picture of a future of promise. They partner together
with strategic managers, like Moses did with Aaron.

Jesus urges his followers to be as street-smart as a cunning manager (Luke 16:1-9) and as shrewd as a serpent (Matthew 10:16). UnLearning leaders study the latest business, leadership, and management models, which is wise.

It's also dangerous. We leaders can become so enamored with business models that we literally adopt everything the corporate world does. We can begin to feel so entitled that we begin to dream about private jets and personal chauffeurs. We start to feel more important and more privileged than other servants in God's church.

Or we become bully-leaders who make critical decisions in churches while we beat up others, verbally or emotionally. Bullies like that keep God's purpose from being accomplished. In Luke 22.25 Jesus had harsh words for people who "lord it over" others.

We must also be careful not to devalue the need for great managers. The megachurch model of the 1990s emphasized the critical need for leadership in the church but rarely mentioned the complementing need for skilled management. We forget how the body of Christ works, how we are connected to each other with complementary gifts in a community of promise.

The only way I live as a person of promise in God's eyes is to be connected. What makes me a member of the body is that I'm connected to Christ. If I'm connected to him, I have to be connected to his people.

I CANNOT BE CONNECTED TO Christ IF I'M NOT CONNECTED TO Christ's people.

Christianity is different from every religion around the globe. All the major world religions focus on the personal quest: "me and God" or "me and the great creative life force" or even "me and nature." Christianity makes another claim:

"Where two or three are gathered in my name, I am there among them," says Jesus (Matthew 18:20).

CHRISTIANITY DOESN'T REVOLVE AROUND ATTENDING MEETINGS BUT AROUND being connected TO PEOPLE OF GOD'S PROMISE.

When I fully give myself to the presence of Christ who is here, when I fully take into myself the presence of Christ who is here, I'm invaded by his life. Through this ongoing encounter, God makes me a person of promise.

I am unLearning the attitude of leading alone or of thinking my gifts to be more important than the contributions of others. I am learning to partner together with managers, like Moses did with Aaron.

GETTING ALONG AT CHURCH

Leaders have a spirit of influence. It's like the law of E.F. Hutton: When God speaks, people listen. Someone in the position of, say, pastor isn't necessarily a leader. Leadership isn't position but a power of God to influence others.

Leaders see God's dream and then enlist people to make it happen. People buy into the credibility of the leader and then into the credibility of the vision.

Leaders have an outward focus. Leaders continually look to the place of promise, as Moses did. Leaders help people picture the place of promise.

MY JOB IS NOT TO MANAGE THE PRESENT SO MUCH AS TO PROCLAIM a future of promise.

Leaders encourage people to continue the journey. They are the point person who is visible and out ahead. They are out front demonstrating faithfulness, fruitfulness, and a commitment to finish well.

Leaders don't put vision up for a vote. They know that people will always vote to go back to Egypt, as they tried under Moses' leadership. Egypt is all many of them have known. The Israelites brought so much baggage and so many pagan traditions from their past that when things got tough for them, they used it all to build an incredible institutional edifice in God's name. All this effort turned out to be nothing more than a golden calf that looked like a god from the land they had just left behind.

UnLearning leaders fear spending their lives
building huge golden calves.

Leaders need strategic managers. The management function has an inward focus. The leader is focused on tomorrow. The manager is concerned with the details for today. Managers are committed to the detailed strategies and logistics to ensure the mission's success. They work together like Moses and Aaron in team.

A person who is a servant-leader is always throwing personal vision forward. The strongest voice Moses heard was the voice of God. He didn't really hear people. Matter of fact, he would disconnect himself from people so he could clearly hear God.

Aaron, on the other hand, did not lead others as much as he managed them. The strongest voice he heard was that of people around him. Managers are so connected to the voice of those around them that they need to hear the vision of the leader, and the leader needs the wisdom of managers who are connected to the people.

There are two kinds of people in the world: pioneers and settlers. Our area of Ohio used to be called the frontier. Many people left places like Philadelphia and Boston and set out for the West Coast. As they got going, they discovered that it was harder than they expected. People became sick and died. Wagon wheels broke.

They got as far as western Pennsylvania and started thinking that Pennsylvania looked rather appealing. All of a sudden these pioneers became settlers. They were paralyzed by the past memory of how good it was in Boston, where they had paved streets and street lamps. Most of the pioneers never got beyond St. Louis.

When you become bogged down
and you quit throwing your light forward, you will settle for
comfort over promise
AND FOR easy over right.

We are drawn to things from the past that reinforce our sense of self-esteem. We become hooked by our past. What would happen if you threw your light forward instead?

For years Chevrolet had trouble with quality. They decided to throw their light forward, so they came up with a slogan: "Like a Rock." They kept advertising that they built their trucks "Like a Rock." Amazingly, what changed were the expectations of the employees at General Motors. They started building a better quality truck.

WHEN LEADERSHIP AND MANAGEMENT

work together,

YOU WON'T WANDER AIMLESSLY IN THE WILDERNESS.

You will look ahead and move forward together.

UnLearning Moment

What is one slogan you are unLearning in order to throw your light forward? For example, people say, "Practice makes perfect," but is that really the attitude you want? How about "risking failure ensures success" instead?

TROUBLE AFOOT

As a leader I tended to downplay the management function. Too many churches I've seen have died because of a management style that had an inward focus. They become controlling, limiting, and visionless.

The churches that grew big during the 1980s and 1990s led from the leadership-CEO side. I did too. When people whined or complained, I asked if they had been baptized. If they said "yes," I replied, "Well, baptism means we're dead, buried, and out of the way. It sounds like someone hasn't held you under the water long enough."

During the summer of 1999, I was out front leading Ginghamsburg to yet another mountain. I looked back and saw grumbling. We had to say goodbye to some staff who were part of the difficulty. We lost two hundred people. For a while, I wondered if I was supposed to stay.

We discovered that leadership and management were moving at different paces. We made some staff adjustments.

I learned that I'm good at vision but terrible at building the details to make the vision happen. I had to find someone who is ahead of me and recruit her to partner with us on staff. I want to be included in the class of leaders who are willing for someone in the organization to be better than they are, and she is. She builds the kinds of teams that help the priesthood of believers happen at Ginghamsburg. Her name is Sue Nilson, and she delights in strategic management. "We view our leadership role as casting directors to find stars whose strengths fit what they are called to do," she says.

Un Learning Moment

What is one un Learning you've recently experienced about leadership and management moving at different paces? What have you done to correct it?

My business card now says my role is Chief Dreamer. I also have a near-identical business card that says Lead Pastor, when I need it for certain denominational meetings.

The church executive team is currently our Creative Director (Kim Miller, quoted several times in this book), the Director of Ministries (Sue Nilson, mentioned above), the Director of New Creation Counseling Center, the Chief Financial Officer/Director of Operations, and the Ginghamsburg Global Director. We're learning how to make leadership and management functions work together.

My gift mix is prophetic teaching (so we're a prophetic-teaching church) and evangelism (so I'm never happy as long as there's one more person out there who needs Jesus). I lie awake at night praying for people to find the fullness of Jesus. But I can't live out those callings alone.

DRUCKER'S THREE QUESTIONS

Everything we do is to help people experience the dynamic love of God in Jesus Christ. What guides us as we connect people to significant relationships and significant responsibilities? Leadership and management expert Peter Drucker often asks people, including church managers and leaders, to consider three questions.[1]

1. What is our business?

In church terms, we might translate that as "What is our mission?"

THE CHURCH'S BUSINESS IS
life transformation.

It's not programs. It's not church-growth numbers. It's not to build brick-and-mortar edifices.

The gospel account of Jesus healing a paralytic demonstrates that the man's four friends clearly understood the business! They carried their friend to Jesus to be healed. Even the Gospel according to Mark (see Mark 2:1-12), for all its brevity, pauses to note that it took four guys to get their sick friend to Jesus. We can't do it alone. In our own paralysis we can't even carry ourselves to Jesus.

Church programs won't change anybody. The only one that has power to create change in our lives is Jesus Christ. That's why we've kept Ginghamsburg from being an issue-centered church.

IT'S OUR GOAL IN ALL WE DO TO
bring people to Jesus.
PEOPLE GROW IN VITAL COMMUNITY.

Notice also that the friend was healed because people felt empowered to serve. Ordinary folks empowered together came up with an innovative idea. "When they could not bring him to Jesus because of the crowd, they removed the roof above him; and after having dug through it, they let down the mat on which the paralytic lay" (Mark 2:4). They had to tear down the existing structure to get their friend to Jesus. Structures have to give way to mission.

2. Who is our customer?

THE CHURCH IS THE ONLY ORGANIZATION ON PLANET EARTH

THAT IS NOT ALLOWED TO
choose its customer.

Jesus' stated mandates are, "I didn't come for the healthy but for the sick" (based on Mark 2:17) and "I've come to seek and save the lost" (based on Luke 19:10).

Once we name Jesus as Lord, we cease being the customer, and we become the missionary. You and I exist solely for the purpose of demonstrating the excellence of God by serving God's purpose here on planet Earth.

At Ginghamsburg we're always about building the next generation. When we forget who our customers are, then we're one generation away from extinction. Our primary customers are twenty-five- to forty-five-year-old people who have children at home. They have been turned off or out by the established church and are interested in pursuing radical faith.

What's my place as someone older than forty-five? Every tribal system and healthy community needs grandparents. My life is sowing seeds that will live on in future generations.

3. What does the customer consider to be of value?

The answer to this question varies from church to church. According to a major survey in our area, people value

    (a) personal life management as it relates to stress,

    (b) parenting skills and help with their children, and

    (c) healthy marriage development.

It's no accident that McDonald's builds playgrounds on the front of their buildings. They understand the felt needs of their customers. Do we?

Radical discipleship is formed in authentic community. Life transformation occurs most readily in biblical community. Discipleship happens as people come together and live in the *koinonia* of the spirit. Healthy Christ-centered community happens when leaders and managers partner together.

One Church That's UnLearning

The Highway Community, Palo Alto, California
www.highway.org

QUICK DESCRIPTION: The Highway Community is a church reaching out to the postmodern culture by practicing truth, authenticity, community, and hope.

HISTORY: Conservative Baptist; Friday night core group started in 1995; Sunday Worship started in 2000.

ATTENDANCE: 225 in one weekend service

THEME: Powerful Synergy Between Leaders and Community

WHAT THE LEADER SAYS: "In reaching the postmodern culture, we have unLearned the traditional trappings of a corporation, which are prevalent in a great deal of American churches. Postmodern people often have a strong distaste for internal structures that remind them of large corporations. We've fashioned the church's internal structure in such a way that we minimize polarization between the congregation and leadership. One way we accomplish this is by avoiding the use of boards and committees. Instead we've set up ministry teams whose meetings consist of worship, prayer, and planning. Managers and leaders partner together when these champions of the ministry teams meet with the pastoral staff for counsel and direction. This happens on a quarterly basis with most individual ministry team meetings. The combination lays the groundwork for a powerful synergy between church leaders and the community of believers at The Highway."

—*John Moser, small group leader since 2000; age late twenties.*

How Are you UnLearning?

- Are you more like the leader or the manager described in this chapter? Give a specific example of what you've had to unLearn to work effectively with your counterpart.

- Draw or paint a picture of what you need to unLearn as you live out Drucker's three questions.

ENDNOTES

1. Peter F. Drucker, *The Essential Drucker* (New York, NY: HarperCollins Publishers, Inc., 2001).

A Higher Value

Speed and information are must-haves for success in the twenty-first century. They are essential to survival, both in the business world and in the church, yet Jesus points us toward a better, higher standard of success.

I was born toward the end of the Industrial Age, which had lasted almost three hundred years.

We're now in the Information Age. When this country was founded, decades would pass before the available knowledge doubled. Today information doubles approximately every eighteen months, and the rate continues to accelerate.

Whether we like it or not, if we're going to survive and compete in the twenty-first century, we must deal with today's commodities of value: speed and information. Everything in today's culture says they are the must-have essentials for success. They are essential to survival, both in the business world and the church, from the workplace to the marketplace.

Think about how these changes affect the way you shop. Ten years ago you didn't take your cell phone shopping with you; most people didn't even have a cell phone. Five years ago virtually no one made a purchase online, but today e-commerce is a multibillion-dollar industry. How many of us have bought a quality computer and found within a year that we have to install an upgrade because it runs too slowly? These are the realities of the twenty-first century.

Our son, Jonathan, plays college baseball. In former days, when college teams would travel for away games, they'd be allowed make-up days for their homework. Now the students are expected to e-mail their assignments from the hotel. Not only do they travel and play ball, but they also have to submit their assignments on the same day they're due for everyone else.

Technology has simplified life, but it also makes life more complex. It allows us to be at work and at play at the same time. It blurs the boundary between the two.

I was in a movie theater with my wife and was distracted by cell phones ringing during the show. Listening in, I couldn't help but notice that people were doing business during the movie. "You've got to close that deal by Wednesday," a man near me was saying.

People in today's high-technology culture have lost the ability to separate business and leisure. They're seeking wealth based on speed and information. No wonder so many people feel an acute need for help with stress management.

A NEW KIND OF WEALTH

Even though Jesus had a heavenly Father of great wealth, he became poor so that through his poverty, you and I would be rich. What a God! The Son of God left infinity and came to this finite planet. Through his poverty, you and I discover wealth.

This wealth isn't only for intelligent or rich people. It's for all people.

This wealth can't be measured through intelligence, beauty, or material prosperity.

This wealth is about transformation.

JESUS' WEALTH IS ABOUT
new life IN HIMSELF.

When we die, God is not going to say, "Well, how much money did you make? How big did you grow your organization? How successful were you in sports or other hobbies?" The number-one question God is going to ask you and me is "What have you done with my Son, Jesus Christ, and the incredible gift of life?"

The purpose of life is not the pursuit of material success and accomplishment.

THE NUMBER ONE PURPOSE IN LIFE IS TO
carry Christ's life EVERYWHERE WE GO.

I'm unLearning certain values that our culture tells us are all-important. We think our hope is the next new car or the bigger house. We keep looking for things to make us feel rich.

Possessions don't give life. You buy a bigger house, which means you have bigger payments, which means you work longer hours, which means you end up spending more time away from your family. Possessions tend to bite us back many times, and they rob us of life. Advertisers forget to tell us about the negative side.

Sometimes I find myself doing things like checking out the worship bulletin and becoming discouraged if the attendance report says we're down from last week. But the secret of life can't be found in that type of success. My hope is in Jesus, who always points us to a higher standard of success than our own.

SPIRIT AND WISDOM AS HIGHER VALUES

Wise people are telescope people who are forever keeping their eyes focused on the future picture. We are constantly searching for what God is doing and adjusting our life purpose accordingly.

Everything around us is shouting speed and information.

UNLEARNING LEADERS UNDERSTAND AND THRIVE IN THESE CHAOTIC WATERS BECAUSE THEY ARE tuned in TO THE SPIRIT'S WISDOM FOR navigating TWENTY-FIRST CENTURY SEAS.

Our spirit is the core of who we are.

While the physical body is degenerating, the spirit should be growing. It's the part of us that lives forever. Spiritual muscles are like physical muscles. When you don't use them, they atrophy. They deteriorate.

I like to ski. I began taking Jonathan out of school for a few days when he was about eleven so we could go to West Virginia to ski.

Soon Jonathan latched on to the idea of skiing in the Rockies. I finally told him that when his basketball season was over, we'd go ski out west together.

Every year before I go skiing, I pull out the stairclimber for a couple of weeks. For the year we were going to the Rockies, I started working out four weeks ahead of time. Jonathan had just finished four months of basketball. It had increased his lung capacity and his leg strength.

One morning we were eating breakfast at home in Ohio, elevation 800 feet, and the next day we were in the Rockies at 11,000 feet. Jon wanted to ski from the top of the mountain, above the tree line, at 13,000 feet.

At the end of the lift, we had to hike up to the top—the place where they never groom the snow. And the mountain was covered with two feet of fresh powder. I was over my knees in powder skiing down, and when you ski in powder, you have to jump. I got down to the tree line and was wiped out! I needed oxygen.

When you're forty-something, you can't expect to get prepared to ski in the Rockies in just four weeks.

The same is true in our walk with God. Most of us have neglected our spirits. UnLearning leaders go beyond the latest leadership fads and technological innovations to the ancient practice of spiritual formation—the practice of daily disciplines that Jesus was committed to, such as prayer, solitude, meditation on the

Word, fasting, commitment to simplicity of lifestyle, service, fellowship, and generous living.

Do you remember the movie *Snow White and the Seven Dwarfs*? It's the story of a beautiful young woman who ate a forbidden fruit and went into a deep sleep. No one could awaken her.

That is what you and I are like when we neglect our spirits. The reality of who we are goes into a sleep, and no one can wake it up, not even the seven vertically challenged friends who hung out with Snow White!

Then a prince came along and awoke her with a kiss. Snow White knew that this was what she was created for.

That is exactly what Jesus Christ does in our lives. Do you remember when you were awakened by Jesus Christ? The manger scene we pull out every Christmas reminds us that while we were sleeping, God kissed us. God loved us and created a plan for us. God wants to restore the broken relationship.

UnLearning Moment

What is one piece of spiritual wisdom that now characterizes your life? Describe what direction you're going and what you're unLearning to get there.

All the energy I put into anything else is going to be gone in a short period of time. But one thing is real: Jesus and what he is doing in my life.

Religion focuses on the outside because outside is what everyone sees. Spirit is what you don't see. That's why it's easy to go so long without paying attention to your spirit. You hurt, and you don't know why. Jesus came to wake us up.

WHEN YOU'RE awakened by Jesus, IT'S ONLY THE BEGINNING OF THE JOURNEY.

DO WHAT YOU KNOW

It's not enough just to be awakened. We've got to decide to follow. Human beings *know* what we *should* do. We *know* what we're *supposed* to do. We must get up and go on the basis of what we already know.

The Magi didn't show up in Bethlehem until two years after the birth of Jesus. Every day for at least twenty-four months, they had to make the decision to continue the journey. Do you think they were ever tempted to stop or go back?

It wasn't enough for them to *know* that Jesus had been born. Don't you think they had days when they found themselves in the middle of the desert and wondered what they were doing?

I was in a rock band in high school. When I joined the group, I knew three chords: C, D, and G. I learned the F chord my second week. I didn't want to waste time by doing the learning first. You do, and then you learn!

THAT'S HOW GOD WORKS TOO.

You follow the star BEFORE YOU ARRIVE AT THE PLACE OF DESTINY.

How many people have been awakened in their relationship with God but still haven't climbed out of bed? Jesus has come and made this incredible announcement that God loves everyone and has a plan for each life, but too many people never really get started.

Real followers get stuck in bed as well. You might need to talk to God, saying, "Lord, this is kind of scary. But I want you to take me to the next level." Then do the next thing. Some of you need to do what you already know.

You don't need to learn new methodologies or clone someone else's ministry model. You need to obey the voice of God's Spirit within you.

We need to remember our spirits. When you do what you know, you grow.

One Church That's UnLearning

Pathways Church, downtown Denver, Colorado
www.pathwayschurch.org

QUICK DESCRIPTION: Helping people engage with God, building relationships that encourage spiritual growth, equipping and releasing followers of Christ to do the work of the ministry, and inviting people to follow Jesus Christ.

HISTORY: Multidenominational, Southern Baptist roots; started in 1995.

ATTENDANCE: five hundred in two services

THEME: Experiencing God's Love Firsthand

UnLearning Church

WHAT THE LEADER SAYS: "We've had to unLearn our thinking about what was needed to reach pre-Christians and to grow Christians. After our first year, we sensed something was wrong. Through listening to different groups of stakeholders, we learned that everyone was in an intensely spiritual community where people could meet God through relationships, worship, service, and art. Most said our biggest strength was the feeling of community that has been growing within the church.

"The rub came at the point of experience. Pre-Christians told us, 'We believe what you are teaching but will not buy in until we experience it.' New Christians said, 'We need more of a sense of transcendence. We want to worship.' Mature Christians asked for more depth in our teaching and more worship.

"We realized that we needed to repackage the church's historic symbols and rituals so that they were more accessible for the present. At the core of who God has made us to be as a church is a very intense desire to live from the heart. We have a very strong culture that cannot be understood merely by watching the mechanics of how we do church. Most of what makes us distinct can only be experienced firsthand."

—*Ron Johnson, church planter and founding pastor of Pathways, has been with the church since its beginning; age late thirties.*

How Are you UnLearning?

- Respond to the last sentence: "When you do what you know, you grow." Give a specific example in the life of someone you are mentoring.

- How have you tasted the price and reward of growing when you do what you know?

148

15

Spiritual visionaries

The CEO model falls short of what a spiritual leader should be. The Christian movement is not based on a professional organizational model. God designed Christianity to be an organic movement of unpaid servants. UnLearning churches are led by chief spiritual visionaries who mobilize lay-based ministry.

When it came time to save the world, God didn't send a professional minister. Jesus was not from the priest tribe of Levi but from Judah. When Jesus spent all night in prayer deciding who should become his leaders to change the world (see Luke 6:12-13), he didn't choose professional clergy. He didn't even select a slate of religious leaders. He called fishermen and tax collectors. None of them could be confused with being professional ministers.

THE ANCIENT CHURCH WAS A lay-based movement.

The institutional church has lost momentum because of its emphasis on professional ministry.

I am unLearning the attitude that clergy should behave like CEOs. Modern business practice, with its professional organizational model, falls too short of what spiritual leadership should be. Jesus intended his followers to be an organic movement of unpaid servants.

UnLEARNING CHURCHES ARE LED BY CHIEF spiritual visionaries WHO MOBILIZE LAY-BASED MINISTRY.

THE NONPROFESSIONAL IN *SAVING PRIVATE RYAN*

Consider the difference in World War II between the Allied forces (including the United States) and the Axis forces (including Nazi Germany). The Allies focused on the platoon leader, who was on the front lines with a small group of about ten or more. He was always moving toward the front, sold out to the mission.

The Axis forces used a strategy of high command that made decisions far from the front line of the ordinary soldier, sometimes as far as Berlin.

In the movie *Saving Private Ryan*, the character played by Tom Hanks isn't a professional soldier. He is an English teacher, drafted for the cause of the mission. Yet you couldn't find a better platoon leader. Tom Hanks represents the nonprofessional soldier who was able to understand and articulate the mission. He made the commitment that he wouldn't stop until he won the war.

The Allied approach is like the lay-based ministry that Jesus established for his church.

Lay partnership is also seen before Jesus' time. The Lord's instruction to Moses was to bring some of the elders "to the tent of meeting, and have them take their place there *with* you" (Numbers 11:16b, emphasis added). Then God said, "I will come down and talk with you there; and I will take some of the spirit that is on you and put it on them; and they shall bear the burden of the people along with you so that you will not bear it all by yourself" (Numbers 11:17).

God's instructions represented the both-and of a strong spiritual leader and a team. The idea was to have lay leaders who share the visionary's spirit.

UnLearning Moment

What is one way you have been unLearning to be a solo leader and learning to model the both-and of strong spiritual leader and a team instead?

Leaders need to be sold out to the cause. If they aren't inspired, they won't be inspiring. People can smell the passion of the Spirit. They need to be inspired as well as informed.

SERVANTS WHO LIVE OUR BUSINESS

We learned in recent years that Ginghamsburg had too many administrative groups, and not everyone leading those groups was being adequately informed.

If a group of attorneys asked me to serve on their board, I'd have to decline because I don't understand their business.

Our area of Ohio is a hub of special-parts manufacturers for the automotive industry. As much as I love cars, I couldn't serve on one of their boards either, even if my best friend chaired the board and personally tried to recruit me. A giant gap exists between someone who likes cars and someone who knows the business well enough to provide leadership counsel.

How many people are on the board of your church without understanding your business? How are your board members being trained on the direction the church needs to go? If we want people who understand postmodern, emerging-church ministry, then we must get some of our brightest, sharpest, Spirit-filled leaders who are willing to make the investment to learn and become experts in our "business."

At Ginghamsburg we reduced our administration to one board of nine people (as allowed according to *The Book of Discipline of the United Methodist Church*, 1996 edition, with permission from the district superintendent), plus our six-person lead team. We looked for three human resource specialists, three people with financial backgrounds, and three people with business development expertise. All had to have the biblical qualities of elders.

They, with our staff executive team, are becoming informed together in the business of postmodern emerging church ministry. Each of these unpaid board members agreed to spend one week of their vacation each year to attend a major national church training event together. This training enables the administrative function of the church to be a force-serving mission, rather than a group of control-seeking people.

The people making the critical decisions for the direction of the church must be *inspired*, *informed*, *empowered*, and *engaged*. They need to breathe our church's strategy: to involve people in the life-transforming process of cell, celebration, and call. (I explain the theology behind cell, celebration, and call in my book *Spiritual Entrepreneurs*, Abingdon Press, 1996, and the practical outworking of them in my book *Out on the Edge*, Abingdon Press, 1998.)

They demonstrate engagement, involvement, and stewardship in their gifts and resources to the rest of the church.

THE SPIRIT OF the leader
IS THE SPIRIT OF the team.
THE SPEED OF THE LEADER IS THE SPEED OF THE TEAM.

I once asked our executive director to provide me with the financial giving statistics for our staff. It turned out that I was the top staff giver, and the next five were our executive leadership team—the point leaders that all of the rest of the paid staff report to. Carolyn and I give well over a tithe of our gross income to the church, and we also give to Campus Crusade for Christ, to seminaries, and to World Vision, through whom we sponsored a child. Many others in the church have similar giving patterns.

You can go only as far as you're demonstrating to those who come after you. Likewise our nine new board members were in the top 10 percent of givers across the entire church.

MULTIPLYING MODELS OF THE REAL THING

Think about the person who first connected you to Jesus Christ. Was it one of your parents? a friend? someone else?

Whenever I take a show-of-hands poll, only a tiny group nominates a professional minister. The vast majority point to an unpaid servant such as a Sunday school teacher, youth leader, small group leader, college friend, contagious neighbor, or co-worker.

THE unpaid servant WILL SPELL
THE SUCCESS OR FAILURE OF THE CHRISTIAN MISSION.

When our church does a leadership conference, drawing hundreds of church leaders from across the United States and many from around the globe, I am most energized by the three hundred unpaid servants right here at Ginghamsburg. They take time off work to use their gifts to serve Christ's mission. After taking note of them, I go home praising God, saying, "They get it!"

You couldn't pay me all the money in the world to travel and speak full time at conferences. I want to connect myself to people at the local level who are willing to give of themselves to be real followers of Jesus Christ. As I examine other churches that reach people today by demonstrating radical Christianity, I sense that same value.

I'd rather have a church of twelve people who can replicate the DNA of the kingdom of God than a church of thousands that will infect people with something less. Choose leaders and managers because they have the ability to influence and replicate the DNA—the core vision and values of the movement of God.

Lay leadership needs to be carefully selected, based first and foremost on Spirit. Others will catch whatever spirit you present.

The kingdom of God is about Spirit, not size. Take time to build the real thing, not watered-down, lukewarm look-alikes. If we're going to be the church at all, let's be the real thing. Build the church God's way: as an organic movement of unpaid servants.

One Church That's UnLearning

Christ Church United Methodist, Fort Lauderdale, Florida
www.christchurchum.org

QUICK DESCRIPTION: The church's three core values are to introduce people to Jesus in positive ways, to disciple believers through Wesley Fellowship Groups, and to relieve suffering in the name of Jesus.

HISTORY: United Methodist; started in 1958.

ATTENDANCE: 1,600 in three weekend services

THEME: Spirit of Leader Is Spirit of Entire Team

WHAT THE LEADER SAYS: "I'm unLearning spiritual leadership. I cannot share what I do not have. My fundamental need is to become a spiritual leader who connects people with God and leads the church into the future. Being a spiritual leader means learning to trust God. It is depending on the God who is still actively redeeming a lost world through Jesus Christ.

"When I don't take the time to grow in this relationship with God, I find myself running on 'empty' and leading out of my own strengths and talents. I need to make my relationship with God the number one priority in my life. The church will never experience renewal without spiritual leaders."

—*Dick Wills, senior pastor, has been with the church since 1986; age fifties.*

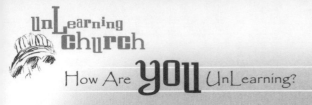
- How are you becoming a spiritual visionary who mobilizes a lay-based movement? What is your role in that process at your church?

- What are some action words that indicate how you will respond?

- Write your dialogue with God in response to this chapter.

Radical Prayer Is About Listening

16

UnLearning leaders are charged by God with the spiritual welfare of a group of people. They must operate out of an intuitive sense of God's direction. Radical prayer goes beyond hearing God to acting on what they hear God say.

Jesus first goes to his heavenly Father in prayer before he attempts a miracle. He follows a clear pattern. He listens to God and then ventures out on what he hears God say. He risks looking stupid.

To the crowd surrounding a dead girl, he says, "The girl is not dead but sleeping" (Matthew 9:24b). The people laugh hysterically: "The man is hopelessly delusional, in a chronic case of denial." Then Jesus raises her from the dead.

To relatives of his dead friend Lazarus, who is buried in a cave sealed by a large rock at the entrance, he says, "Take away the stone" (John 11.39a). While everyone is preparing to deal with the putrid stench of a decaying corpse, Jesus commands the dead man, "Lazarus, come out!" (John 11:43b).

JESUS' MINISTRY DEMONSTRATES THAT acting on what God says WILL BE messy.

God's miracles come in the form of seeds. Too many Christians are waiting around for mature, ripe fruit, but God doesn't hand out mature, ripe fruit. You must first put seeds into the ground before anything can grow. You must act on your conviction, your intuitive sense of what God is saying.

God has charged me as a pastor with the spiritual welfare of a group of people. Prayer is such an intimate connection that I can't explain it in steps A to Z. CUTE, CHURCHY definitions and formulas ONLY TRIVIALIZE PRAYER.

The best thing I can do is challenge people to experience it.

Prayer will be different for each person. But prayer for all is intimate awareness of God's presence. Prayer is connecting to our deepest longing.

Sometimes I have Big Mac attacks in which I get a food pictured in my mind and can't get it out. I've gotten out of bed at night to fix myself a pastrami sandwich. I go to bed thinking I'll have it for lunch the next day and then can't wait. My body is craving food, and I act on that desire.

We actually have a deeper longing—an intimate, connective need for the presence of God. Just as our bodies crave food, our spirits long to be fed. Only an intimate relationship with God can fill that spiritual hunger.

Real change and transformation come through commitment to radical prayer. It is so easy to forget the relational connection with God. Prayer is not some simple, little formula. It goes much further than the little nod-to-God kind of spiritual aerobics that a lot of us habitually fall into.

A few years ago, when I was in the Himalayan mountains, I heard this expression: "When the explorer is ready, the guide will come." Prayer is our willingness to connect to the guide. When we come to that place in our spiritual journey, it is indescribable. I can't give you a prescriptive formula for prayer. All I can describe is the essential necessity to set aside all distractions and daily enter a quiet place to intuitively listen. Listening is what prayer is about.

I'M UNLEARNING THE APPROACH TO PRAYER
MARKED BY one-way talking
OR RECITING SELF-DIRECTED WISH LISTS.

I'm moving to the kind of radical prayer that senses the will of God and does it. Without this intuitive sense of direction, I will not grow as an individual or leader of God's church.

GLOBAL, LOCAL, AND PERSONAL PRAYER

Have you ever felt that your issues were not significant enough for God's involvement—that God deals only with big things? "If people are starving in the world, how can God possibly be concerned about my bad-hair days?" Yet the Bible bears the claim that God knows how many hairs are left on my head and even cares if a bird falls out of its nest.

I'M UNLEARNING
MY relationship WITH GOD.

I'm discovering that God wants to be intimately involved in the details. God waits to be invited into my personal spaces.

For years Wendy and her husband, Roger, had wanted a baby. They went to doctors who specialized in fertility. They did everything they could think of with no results. One evening when they were visiting our home, we decided to pray about their need. We stood around Wendy and prayed for her. Three weeks later she found out she was pregnant with twins.

God's answers aren't always so obvious or straightforward. Sometimes God will answer a prayer like that by opening up some wonderful opportunities through adoption. Jesus said, "If you abide in me, and my words abide in you, ask for whatever you wish, and it will be done for you" (John 15:7). What a promise! What a God!

PRAYER LEADS TO INTIMATE AWARENESS

Everything Jesus does is dependent upon his relationship with the Father. Jesus told people, "I tell you, the Son can do nothing on his own, but only what he sees the Father doing; for whatever the Father does, the Son does likewise" (John 5:19b). Before he began his public ministry, he spent forty days communing with God through prayer and fasting.

The Psalms describe how David longed for an intimate experience of God. "O God, you are my God, I seek you, my soul thirsts for you; my flesh faints for you, as in a dry and weary land where there is no water" (Psalm 63:1).

In what ways do you connect intimately with God? In the pace of ministry, it's easy to anesthetize our need to intimately connect with God. What David says is that ultimately our deepest longing, our real hunger, the intimacy we crave is an intimate connectedness to God. Prayer leads us to that intimate connectedness.

Prayer requires listening intently because God is talking. The sense of intimate awareness will be different for each of us, but in the moment of connection, we become aware that God is speaking, and we're hearing what God is saying. I'm aligning my thoughts with God's thoughts and my actions with God's actions.

PRAYER IS
thinking and moving WITH GOD.

Prayer is not a formula; it is straining forward, as somebody committed to the rigorous exercise of mountaineering. Climbing is an ongoing process of making commitments and moving forward. You have to take one foothold at a time, one

handhold at a time, and then the next, and the next. To get off a plateau in any area of your life, you must make the commitment to move forward.

PRAYER IS ABOUT LISTENING

Sometimes on Monday, our day off, Carolyn and I sit in the kitchen in the morning and drink coffee. I read the newspaper, and we talk. One day she was trying to tell me about her mom being sick. Right in the middle of Carolyn recounting her conversation with her mother, I said, "Oh, Carolyn, look at this. Did you read this in the paper?" I talked right over her. I hadn't really been listening to her.

Most of the time, what we call prayer is talking over God.

TOO OFTEN WHEN WE PRAY,

GOD IS SPEAKING,

AND we aren't listening.

We're following our agenda and talking over God.

Jesus understood that prayer is about listening. Luke tells us that while Jesus was praying, heaven opened and he heard the voice of God. (See Luke 3:21.)

WHEN YOU REALLY PRAY,

YOU WILL BE connecting TO WHAT GOD IS SAYING.

God spoke to the prophets long ago, and they faithfully recorded the teachings in the books we know as the Bible. But God didn't stop speaking between the first and second centuries A.D.

Jesus told the early church, "I still have many things to say to you, but you cannot bear them now. When the Spirit of truth comes, he will guide you into all the truth; for he will not speak on his own, but will speak whatever he hears, and he will declare to you the things that are to come" (John 16:12-13). God wants to direct you into his future with a new word each day. It's essential to create God-listening moments in every day of our lives.

Once when I was on the road for a seminar, I had to do the technical setup myself. Dealing with technical "stuff" is a major drain for me. My solution was to get up two hours early so I could listen to God in prayer. It worked. I was ready to unpack the box with its cables, switches, and computer tower.

Where do I find life? In today's word from God. In today's direction.

Danger lurks when I am not creating God-listening moments in my life. I fall into the trap of religion. *Religion* is yesterday's word.

RELIGION BECOMES A LIFE OF NOTHING MORE THAN

rules and regulations.

It always becomes stale bread, stagnant prayers, and old advice. There is no life in religion.

New Christians demonstrate excitement and new life that comes from a fresh, dynamic relationship with Jesus. I always warn them, "Don't get religious." When they hang around religious people who don't have a fresh word from God, all they learn are rules and regulations, and they so quickly become like the critical, negative scribes of Jesus' day.

PRAYER TAKES US BEYOND "SHOULD"

All of us have made resolutions. Most people who lose weight gain it back. Most people who are released from prison go back to prison. Why don't resolutions work? It is because they are based on *should*. "I should do this." Should is often the "have to" that other people put on us. It is an outside-in approach.

I went to the doctor for a physical one spring, and my cholesterol was a little high. He told me that I should go on a low-fat diet. I walked out of the office agreeing, "I should." I went home and became serious about it. I began to read about how I'd have to eat a lot of fish and chicken. I learned that chocolate is bad and potato chips had to go. I began to check labels for the number of fat grams.

Resolutions are based on *should*. I was becoming a student of diet because the doctor told me that I should. For six weeks I was serious about what I should do. I was so good.

Then one day in the sixth week, I came to work and passed a friend's workstation. I saw some McDonald's french fries there. I thought I'd just eat three french fries, but I ate them all. That moment was the end of my low-fat diet.

That's the problem with resolutions. They are based on *should*—external things that other people put on us. The doctor told me I should.

Listening prayer BRINGS US

TO A PLACE WHERE WE ARE NO LONGER LIVING OUT OF

RESOLUTIONS OR *SHOULD*.

Resolutions lack power because they are based on our will, which is not strong enough to promote lasting change. Emerging church leaders live out of a deep awareness of the call of God. Jesus said, "The words that I have spoken to you are spirit and life" (John 6:63b). When we are tracking with God and acting with God, it is no longer a matter of *should*; it becomes a matter of *must*.

I have an urgency in my life. I've got to do it. I am wired to do it. I can't help but do it.

PRAYER WALKS IN GOD'S COUNSEL

We are committed to our children, and we are imperfect. We would give our lives for their success. How much more will God do, who wants to guide you to the place of promise for your life?

RADICAL PRAYER IS BOLDLY

risking forward.

God desires your success and the fulfillment of your created purpose. God cares as the perfect parent.

We often think of prayer as a complicated game of Hide-and-Seek, like God is hiding from us. If you are a parent, do you go out and hide from your kids? If they are stumbling around, trying to find direction, do you hide and let them run into the wall? No. You give guidance and clear direction to your children.

When our daughter, Kristen, was in her senior year of college, she began applying to graduate schools. Her field of dietetics and nutrition is very competitive, so she was a little nervous. Being a dad, I did everything I knew to give her a competitive edge. I called her on the phone: "Kristen, e-mail your essays to me, and let me help with the sound bites to make your essay sound better." I also advised her on how to handle interviews with aggressive confidence. As her dad, I wanted to make available to Kristen the collective wisdom that comes from my almost fifty years of experience. We were on the phone for hours, and it was my dime, not hers.

If I as an imperfect parent—a broken person—desire to give all my wisdom and counsel to my children, how much more does God want to guide those who ask? That's what radical prayer is about. God desires our best so much "that he gave his only Son" (John 3:16a)—his own life, that you and I might succeed.

We're not going forward until we commit ourselves to radical prayer that compels us to risk forward in the counsel of God.

PRAYER LEADS TO COSTLY ACTION

Radical prayer is not just hearing God. Radical prayer results in radical action. It is doing what you hear God say. The Bible says God is looking for people to speak to and bless. Not because they're brilliant but because they are willing to do whatever God says. "Blessed rather are those who hear the word of God and obey it!" (Luke 11:28).

Imagine living in a desert climate where it doesn't rain even three inches a year, and God says, "Build a boat 450 feet long, 75 feet wide, and 45 feet high." The directive to Noah didn't make sense. How was Noah going to find that much wood in the desert? Where would he acquire the financial backing, supplies, and workers that would be needed? But as a servant of God, Noah said, "It doesn't matter if it doesn't make sense, God. Here I am, use me." His reply was something like that because the Bible records, "Noah did all that the Lord had commanded him" (Genesis 7:5).

A postmodern movie called *The Matrix* uses a lot of biblical symbolism. Its physical fights compare to the spiritual fights with evil that go on today. Neo has a mission to do, and God is contacting Neo through a man named Morpheus. The following dialogue begins as Neo, in his cubicle at work, answers a cell-phone call.

> **Morpheus:** Hello, Neo, do you know who this is?
>
> **Neo:** Morpheus?
>
> **Morpheus:** Yes, I've been looking for you, Neo. I don't know if you're ready to see what I want to show you, but unfortunately you and I have run out of time. They're coming for you, Neo...
>
> **Neo:** What...do they want from me?
>
> **Morpheus:** I don't know. But, if you don't want to find out, you better get out of there.
>
> **Neo:** How?
>
> **Morpheus:** I can guide you out, but you must do exactly as I say.
>
> **Neo:** OK.
>
> **Morpheus:** The cubicle across from you is empty. Go! now!

Neo dashes across the small hallway and hides in an empty work area. His journey has many parallels to how God leads followers of Jesus. God tells us, "Listen and do it. I can guide you, but you must do exactly as I say. Do it now." God also contacts people in unusual ways.

Neo continues to listen to the voice that symbolizes spiritual presence.

Morpheus: When I tell you, go to the end of the row to the first office on the left. Stay as low as you can. Now. Good. Now there is a window. Open it.

Neo: How do you know all this?

Morpheus: The answer is coming, Neo. Outside, there's a scaffold. You can use it to get to the roof.

Neo: No! It's too far away.

Morpheus: There's a small ledge. It's a short climb. You can make it.

Neo: No way. Now way. This is crazy.

Morpheus: Don't be controlled by your fear, Neo. There are only two ways out of this building. One is that scaffold. The other is in their custody. You take a chance either way. I leave it to you.

Neo: This is insane! Why is this happening to me? What did I do?

Like Jesus' disciple Peter who walked on water while he kept his eyes on Jesus, Neo took his eyes away from his source and looked down. Like God, Morpheus says he can't explain everything. Morpheus' message is "You've got to trust me. I can't explain it to you." Walking with God does not always make sense and is not rational. Like us, Neo has two choices, two ways out: the radical, higher, and costly way of finding the will of God and doing it, or going out in the custody of the forces of this world that will create a series of distractions until you die.

One of Jesus' stories about watchfulness warns us to "be dressed for action and have your lamps lit; be like those who are waiting for their master to return from the wedding banquet, so that they may open the door for him as soon as he comes and knocks" (Luke 12:35-36).

What time is it for God's people? Notice the image of awake, waiting, and alert when the master comes. "If he comes during the middle of the night, or near dawn, and finds them so, blessed are those slaves" (Luke 12:38). We are first and foremost servants of God.

THE ENEMY'S PURPOSE IS TO
distract us
TO A LOWER LEVEL OF LIVING
until we die.

Jesus says, "You also must be ready, for the Son of Man is coming at an unexpected hour" (Luke 12:40).

PRAYER THAT LEADS INTO THE UNKNOWN

The currents of cultural change are so unpredictable that it's impossible to strategically plan five or ten years ahead. UnLearning leaders are prepared to follow Christ's voice fearlessly into a future of promise.

People often ask about my five- or ten-year plan for Ginghamsburg. "Where will the church be in a decade?" they're interested to know. I don't have such a plan. If I were the one in charge, I'd have a plan. But I'm not a corporate CEO. I'm following Jesus. He is my life. He knows the future. I don't know which way he will turn. I can only follow.

Change is accelerating at an exponential pace, and it is impossible to accurately predict five to ten years into the future. We've learned to focus on one-year plans. "We seek God for a big picture and then build it as we go," explains Sue Nilson.

In 1994 when I was praying in Korea, I had this picture of 10,000 people being at Ginghamsburg by the year 2000. When I came back, I risked sharing the vision with the people. In 1999 I began to ask myself, "What if it doesn't happen?" I'm now finishing this book in 2001. On-campus attendance has grown but hasn't reached anywhere close to 10,000. (We did reach well over 10,000 via the Internet, which wasn't even a possibility back in 1994!)

I would rather apologize than ask for permission. I'm not ashamed of following God's picture. Jesus' disciple Peter didn't worry about failure or fearing what people thought. He said, "Lord, if it is you, command me to come to you on the water" (Matthew 14:28).

I was with my friend Len Sweet, who wrote the foreword to this book. He was speaking to pastors, and he called Ginghamsburg the "Velcro church." I wondered what he meant.

Len, who has been dean and president of a theological school explained: He had once brought a group of graduate students to our campus. They were touring our facility and walked past the prayer rooms on either side of the sanctuary. As they went by, the students noticed a sign outside each room: "in use/available." The sign is held on by Velcro. The tour guide moved the sign from "available" to "in use," but it immediately fell to the floor. The tour guide picked it up and tried to reattach it, but it fell again. The same thing happened a third and fourth time.

When the students returned to school, they discussed what they learned from Ginghamsburg. They noticed that when the prayer sign was hung on the "in use" side, it would not stick because the Velcro had worn out. "Somebody is praying," they concluded.

People who pray understand. It is not the trees that move the wind, but wind moves the trees. It is not matter that moves spirit, but spirit that moves matter.

GREAT PRAYER

Belief doesn't become faith until we act on God's directive. Before you can lead others, you first must be able to lead yourself.

The key to self-leadership and self-discipline is a lifestyle of prayer. When you are out on the edge, attempting the impossible, you can't help but live in an atmosphere of prayer.

THE LIFE OF AN UNLEARNING LEADER REQUIRES total dependence UPON GOD.

Look at the prayers of our Lord. As Jesus prayed the night before his death, he didn't say, "God, please, make this as painless as possible." Put into today's language, he said, "This is going to cost me everything."

What if you knew that following Jesus Christ would cost you your life? Would you turn to another teacher or ideology to help you become self-actualized? Or would you be willing to go the way of ultimate sacrifice to fulfill God's purpose?

Greatness does not say, "Please, God, save me." Greatness says, "God, whatever it takes, use me for your purpose and pleasure."

One Church That's UnLearning

Vineyard Community Church, Cincinnati, Ohio
www.cincyvineyard.com and www.servantevangelism.com

QUICK DESCRIPTION: Vineyard Community Church in Cincinnati is pioneering the planting of multiple outward-focused churches each year. They have pioneered the concept of servant evangelism to reach their city.

HISTORY: Vineyard; started in 1983.

ATTENDANCE: 5,500 in five weekend services

THEME: Learning to Listen in Prayer

WHAT THE LEADER SAYS: "We exist to love our city into relationship with Christ. Prayer is the doorway that opens up God's activity in and around our lives. Those who expect God to answer often see amazing things happen.

"I've been learning how to lead our congregation to be a unique people of prayer. We've unLearned the devotional approach of having a 'Quiet Time,' which I learned in my college fellowship. We've moved toward simple, more experimental approaches. Our most emphasized prayer is ministry prayer: hands-on prayer for others, asking God to touch, heal, and empower individuals. We also do a lot of intercessory prayer for our city, church, and specific needs. We encourage times of complete quietness enhanced by wearing headphones in order to just listen to God. We also practice 'driving prayer'—instead of listening to the radio while in our cars, we tune into God by praying in the Spirit on the way to work and get in touch with the presence of God for the day.

"Listening in prayer is more important than talking."

—Steve Sjogren, launching pastor, has been with the church since its beginning; age mid-forties.

How Are **you** UnLearning?

- Describe your journey of stripping yourself of anything that impedes your walk with God.

- In your own experience, what does radical prayer and action feel like? What color symbolizes this feeling?

- Consider if you can sincerely pray this prayer: "Here I am, God. Everything I have is for your pleasure and your purpose. Amen."

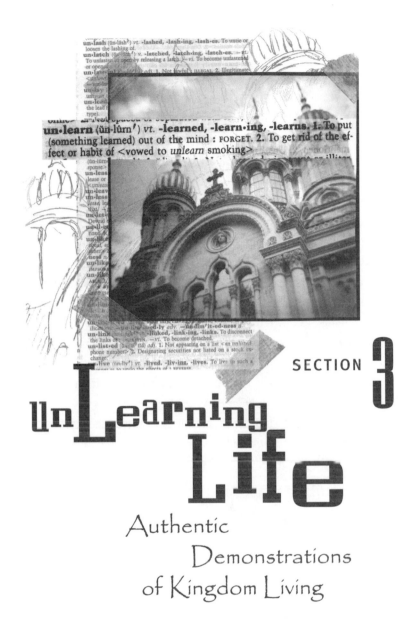

SECTION **3**

Un**L**earning **Life**

Authentic
Demonstrations
of Kingdom Living

The One Thing

When you live for the purpose of pleasing God, it will bless and benefit others. Why trade the continuum of eternity for the "kingdom of scratch"?

Jesus ended his thirty-three-year life on earth by saying, in effect, "Father, it is completed. I've finished the one thing you sent me to do." (See John 17:4; 19:28.) Jesus was faithful to his life purpose all the way to the finish line.

The world invites us to do everything and go everywhere. The surrounding culture wants us to believe we have lots of time to try anything and everything.

Time is a precious commodity that we cannot buy more of. We get one opportunity, one life, and when we die we don't get a chance for a do-over. Each of us has been uniquely created and wired by God to give himself or herself to one primary thing. Everything in life comes down to the call that God has for each of us. I keep telling my children that in spite of popular opinion, they have time in life to give themselves for only one great purpose.

Being a dad and husband is the most important thing God has called me to do. Being a good friend to my wife is more important than leading the church, and what happens in our children's lives is critical to Carolyn and me.

I'M HAVING TO UNLEARN CERTAIN POPULAR VALUES TO BECOME A *living demonstration* OF GOD'S "ONE THING" FOR ME: PUTTING *God first*, FAMILY SECOND, AND CAREER OR CHURCH NEXT.

It's easy for me as a local pastor to begin to think life is about building a church program, financial budget, or staff team. I'm also tempted to think life revolves around the numbers associated with church growth.

Instead, we are in the business of transformational discipleship—life change.

OUR BUSINESS PRODUCT IS REVOLUTIONARY— PEOPLE WHO HAVE BEEN INVADED BY THE *supernatural force* OF THE HOLY SPIRIT.

UnLearning leaders are not replicating the values of the surrounding culture but are demonstrating the radical, countercultural life of the kingdom of God.

Nothing less than full devotion to God and God's purpose for my life will do as my "one thing."

Pleasing God

IS THE MOST IMPORTANT VALUE I CAN MODEL AS A LEADER.

It's what Jesus was about: "The one who sent me is with me; he has not left me alone, for I always do what is pleasing to him" (John 8:29).

BAIT AND SWITCH

When you live for the purpose of pleasing God, it will bless and benefit others and bring you joy. Why trade the continuum of eternity for what my friend Wayne Cordeiro calls "the scratch"?

Cordeiro is a church leader in Hawaii and author of *Doing Church as a Team*. He paints a vivid word picture of what it means to live a small life. He says to imagine a cable stretched in front of you that extends in both directions beyond what the eye can see. The cable represents a continuum that goes into eternity.

To contrast the brevity of our earthly existence with that of eternity, I would take out my ballpoint pen and draw a vertical scratch on the extended cable. Then I would tell you that the width of that scratch mark (about ½ of an inch) represents how long our life on Earth is in comparison with eternity. Not very long!

But do you know what most people do? They not only live on that scratch, but they also love that scratch. They kiss the scratch. They save for that scratch. They hoard for that scratch. They live scratch lives, have scratch businesses and have scratch families with scratch hopes and scratch dreams.

But God so loved that scratch that He sent His only begotten Son to die for those who live there. Yet many still don't know about this gift called eternal life! They're still hanging on to the scratch. They try to elongate it, stretch it and extend it as much as possible. But even in the midst of their attempts, they know deep inside that there's got to be something more.[1]

Yet we continue to focus on the scratch. We have little-scratch dreams, drive little-scratch cars, live in little-scratch homes, and raise little-scratch children.

When we die, we leave behind little-scratch accomplishments.

A friend of mine told me that he needed a boat. "I've worked hard all my life, and I deserve it," he said. "I need something that will help me get away from it all."

He took the boat out twice last year and made twelve payments. Talk about diminishing returns! You end up serving whatever kingdom you buy into.

What is the lure of these kingdoms? Each is an enticement to pleasure, prestige, or possessions. A shortcut to a promising future. A compromise from authentic life values. That's what Satan implied to Jesus: "Here is the world, exactly what you came for." (See Matthew 4:1-11, Luke 4:1-13.) The world was Jesus' goal when he came to earth: "God sent his only Son into the *world* so that we might live through him" (1 John 4:9b, emphasis added).

"Guess what, Jesus?" Satan's argument continues. "My offer even comes with a shortcut to what you are looking for. You can have the world without the costly inconvenience of life sacrifice. All you have to do is worship me first."

That's the catch.

LIFE ISN'T ABOUT personal pleasure; IT IS ABOUT pleasing God.

Jesus was clear about his one thing. "Worship the Lord your God, and serve only him" (Matthew 4:10b). "Everything else is only scratch!" If you want to fulfill your God destiny, you must fully commit your life purpose and resources to the one thing that God has created you for.

Jesus came out of the wilderness after forty days of testing. Jesus' next recorded words affirmed again, "This is why I was sent: to serve God. This is my one thing." (See Luke 4:18-19.) Later Luke uses the word picture of Jesus setting his face toward Jerusalem. (See Luke 9:51-53.) Jerusalem was not a prestigious retirement community on a golf course or the place where he would experience the notoriety of a successful megaministry. Jerusalem was where Jesus would give his life for the life of the world.

UnLearning Moment

What is one way you have been unLearning your own life purpose?

Remember the movie *Chariots of Fire*? It tells the story of Eric Liddell, the son of a missionary, who was also a tremendous athlete. He agonized over whether he should prepare as a runner for the 1924 Paris Olympics. "I've decided, I'm going back to China," he told his sister Jenny in one poignant scene, as the two of them walked along the hills of their native Scotland. "The missionary society has accepted me."

"I'm so pleased," she replied.

"I've got a lot of running to do first, Jenny," Eric continued.

Jenny didn't understand. She thought running was nothing more than a distraction from ministry.

"You've got to understand," he explained. "I believe God made me for a purpose—for China. [But] he also made me fast.

WHEN I RUN, I FEEL HIS PLEASURE.

To give it up WOULD BE TO HOLD HIM IN CONTEMPT.

You are right; it's not just fun. To win is to honor him."

Why do we run? Why do we do ministry? Why do we do anything? To give God pleasure.

WHEN YOU LIVE FOR THE PURPOSE OF PLEASING GOD,
YOUR LIFE WILL honor God; BLESS AND BENEFIT OTHERS;
AND, BETTER THAN PLEASURE, BRING YOU JOY.

Why would anyone trade the kingdom of eternity for a kingdom of scratch?

AS LEADERS, OUR MOST AUTHENTIC DEMONSTRATION
OF KINGDOM LIVING CAN BE SEEN IN OUR
daily tasks and relationships.

UnLearning leaders don't aspire to fit in with the bland and tasteless religiously correct. They fully give themselves to a movement of God that is bold and contagious. Our lives become our message.

THE LIMITS OF OTHERS

In April of 1979, when I came to the little white-clapboard and brick country church known as Ginghamsburg, I knew all the church's godfathers and godmothers would have an opinion about the direction we should be taking as a church. I went back into the open field behind our building and told God that I would stay there as long as was necessary. "What is *your* purpose, God?" I prayed. "What is

your pleasure for this church?" On that day I pictured a spiritual center where more than three thousand people would worship and where people would come from around the world to experience God's blessing. I also dreamed of a future in which we would model racial reconciliation among both our leadership and our people.

I learned never to wait for other people to tell me what I should do with my life because their ideas will be smaller than God's creative intent. I experienced the importance of personal involvement in prayer, as I see and commit myself to heaven's picture for my life.

WELL-INTENTIONED BEGINNINGS

How many of us start something and never finish it? You might start exercising or dieting, and then the holidays come. You give in to the enticement of the moment, and you never realize the completion of your dream. Debt becomes a problem. When you are always working to pay the past, you never have resources to sow to God's future. You may be convinced that credit-card debt doesn't honor God, but Christmas, a vacation dream, or someone's birthday comes, and you yield. You never grasp the fulfillment of God's purpose.

In 1863 the pastor who founded Ginghamsburg had a vision. God spoke, and twenty people made a commitment to Christ in the congregation's first two weeks of life. The pastor's vision was that from this tiny, little church, a spiritual revival would begin that would ultimately touch the world.

God is fulfilling that vision. Each month more than 50,000 people are touched through our Web site. Our twice-annual Change Conference typically draws up to a thousand people—from across the United States and usually from ten or more different countries. In November of 2000, The Wall Street Journal did an article on Ginghamsburg Church. We've received citations from the White House and recognition from the Christian press.

That pastor had a vision in 1863, so why did it take 138 years to be realized? Because no pastoral leader stayed more than five years. Every time a pastor faced resistance, he left and went to another place.

I remember what Mike Lyons, a former staff person and friend at Ginghamsburg, said to me. "I've been part of this church the whole time you have, and you've done nothing great in any one year." Then he explained with a smile, "You simply don't go away."

What does that kind of endurance say for the long-term effect of parenting? What does it say for the potential hidden in a marriage? What does it say for our church's mission to reach our community? God's promise can be fulfilled in your life when you are willing to stay there, stick at it, and commit your whole life to it.

I've been tempted several times to leave Ginghamsburg before the vision God has given me is fully accomplished. God's miracle will not happen if I do not persevere through the promise.

FEAR OF RISK

It seems that the older we become, the harder we work at staying comfortable. But it wasn't always so. When you were a child and you saw a puddle of water, what was your tendency? You jumped in the middle of it! What do adults do? We don't want to mess up our shoes or get wet, so we try to walk around the puddle. Fearing discomfort, we stay as dry as possible.

When I was growing up, I loved to play around a creek in the woods behind our house. Any time I'd go outside, my mom would tell my friends and me to stay out of the creek. Her warning usually didn't keep us from playing *over* the creek, however. We challenged each other to swing out on a rope swing as far as we could from one side of the creek to the other, hanging on to that long rope and then dropping safely onto the other bank.

One day right after a rain, we were swinging across the creek. The creek was full—the best time to swing across! Unfortunately, I didn't let go at quite the right time. I came backward over the water again, and before I knew it, I was in water up to my knees.

Soaking wet, I trotted home. I owned only two pairs of blue jeans. My mom told me to put on the dry pair but warned me that if I got wet again, I'd get the whupping of my life.

I went back to the creek in my last pair of jeans, intending only to watch the other kids. But when you're a child, you're willing to take risks. I saw the rope, the rushing creek, and my friends in action. I thought, "Whupping or stay dry on the bank, watching?" I knew I could make it. I grabbed the rope and swung across. Attempting to keep my pants clean, I raised my feet up high. I made it to the other side but didn't drop my feet and plant them fast enough. I began to teeter and then changed directions. As I swung back over the creek, I put my feet up high again—causing me to dip into the creek back-end first.

When I arrived home the second time, I wasn't wet just from the knees down; I was drenched from the chest down, and my destiny was clear.

Why is it that the older we get, the less elastic we become? Perhaps we've acquired the experience of accumulated butt-whuppings. We realize the cost and become hesitant to move out of safe spaces. God designed us to be co-creators, but we become less daring as we grow older. We cease risking and rest on our laurels.

It's time to reclaim whose you are, for you are not your own. Life is not about downsizing dreams as you age until you arrive at that day of retirement. We're children of today. Our work is to continue the work of Jesus Christ on planet Earth by staying focused on our "one thing." Doing so gives my leadership added credibility and authenticity.

YOUR ONE THING

Jesus said to love the Lord with all our heart, soul, mind, and strength. (See Matthew 22:34-40; Mark 12:28-34; and Luke 10:25-28.) Our relationship with Jesus must be all-consuming. It impacts everything we do. It affects all we are and have.

Jesus sums up the whole Christian life when he says, "Abide in me" (John 15:4a) and "Love one another as I have loved you" (John 15:12b).

Your mission is the mission of Jesus, but in all probability your "one thing" isn't my "one thing." God has wired you uniquely.

YOUR DISTINCT gift mix IS CRITICAL TO GOD'S MISSION AND PURPOSE.

You are an awesome piece of work, designed and inspired by God. Satan's bait and switch seeks to convince you that you are less than everyone else.

The most important impact you can have comes from focusing on the "one thing"—*your* thing.

WILL YOU GIVE YOUR LIFE WITH
courage and boldness,
REGARDLESS OF THE COST,
TO SERVING YOUR UNIQUE MISSION IN THE WORLD?

Don't spend another day living for scratch. As people baptized into Christ, we are dead, buried, and out of the way. Our future is about God's pleasure, not about what you and I want.

As you and I embrace these qualities in expanding measure, our lives will be compelling and authentic to others. What is it about your relationship with Jesus that your community cannot live without knowing? People are looking for real people who model the real deal. Be one.

One Church That's

UnLearning

Westside King's Church, Calgary, Alberta, Canada
www.wkc.org

QUICK DESCRIPTION: A community of people discovering their destiny in relationship to God and others as they move away from traditional paradigms of religion and toward an authentic relationship with the resurrected Christ.

HISTORY: Pentecostal Assemblies of Canada; planted by Calgary's First Assembly of God in 1994.

ATTENDANCE: 1,700 people in four weekend services

THEME: Focusing on the Journey

WHAT THE LEADER SAYS: "We feel like we've had to unLearn everything about doing church. We had to start over and strip off the cultural baggage that was stopping people from entering into the journey with us. The statistics are alarming: A high percentage of people in our city believe in God and Jesus, yet a low percentage attend any community of faith. Instead of church and faith being reduced to an event, we saw that it was inviting people to a journey. With this paradigm shift, worship is no longer a service but a lifestyle. The journey is a major theme for us, and at the deepest level, the shift is from the event of doing church to the journey of a Christ-centered faith and becoming church.

"Our vision is to be a church for people who do not go to church. We want to do church in such a way as to be a safe place for people to do the journey."

—*Tom Morris, pastor, has been with the church since its beginning; age early forties.*

- What is your "one thing"?

- What must you unLearn to be a person of greater impact? What are the first two steps on your journey?

ENDNOTES

1. Wayne Cordeiro, *Doing Church as a Team* (Ventura, CA: Regal Books, 2001), 25.

Picture Day

You become what you look at. If your starting point is wrong, every choice you make after it will be wrong. So identify a healthy life picture that will remind you who you are and whose you are.

Jesus came to earth to reconnect us to the intimacy of experiencing God in everyday life. In Luke 24 two disciples of Jesus were making the seven-mile walk from Jerusalem to a town called Emmaus. Jesus had risen from the grave and joined their journey, but they didn't recognize him. "As they came near the village to which they were going, he walked ahead as if he were going on. But they urged him strongly, saying, 'Stay with us' " (Luke 24:28-29a).

SOMETHING HAPPENS WHEN YOU COME TO
that vulnerable place
WHERE YOU INVITE JESUS INTO THE PLACES WHERE YOU'RE LIVING.

It happens even when you don't fully understand who Jesus is.

When I got serious for the first time, I said, "Jesus, I don't even know if you're there, but if you are, I need you." It's amazing what happens when you pray that kind of prayer. When I took one step toward God, God took two steps toward me. It is amazing how God is more intently interested in connecting with us than we are with him.

When Jesus' earliest disciples invited Jesus into their personal spaces, "their eyes were opened, and they recognized him; and he vanished from their sight" (Luke 24:31).

A group of youth and adult leaders from our church went to Mexico on a mission trip and had an eye-opening encounter. They came back saying, "We've seen the Lord!" Many of us have had that kind of Jesus-recognition experience. People who have these reality-changing experiences can't wait to tell other people about them.

But Jesus vanished from the disciples' sight, according to Luke. These kinds of experiences have a tendency to fade. They will be few and far between, as the disciples quickly discovered. You and I want a Jesus with skin, a Savior we can see. We trust what we can see. We don't trust what we can't see. That's why our initial burst of enthusiasm may begin to fade. After a while we plateau and even stop growing spiritually.

We often trade our intimate relationship with God for service for God. Ginghamsburg is a great serving church. Hundreds of our people give themselves tirelessly to serving God each week.

But serving God IS NOT OUR GREATEST NEED.

An experience of God's presence is key to staying vital for life.

I'm unLearning what it means to be intimate with God and learning to allow my service to be an expression of that relationship. This dynamic is essential to my picture of who I am and whose I am.

UnLearning Moment

How do you feel when you hear, "Serving God is not our greatest need"? What have you had to unLearn over the years about your relationship with God?

TOUCHING THE INVISIBLE

One Easter my entire extended family came to our home. My mom said to me, "Michael, did you ever have a time in your life when you knew Jesus was there? I mean *physically* there with you?" She went on to reflect about attending a family camp I was leading in Wilmore, Kentucky, in the summer of 1974. She recalled her own experience: "I was standing in a circle, holding hands with a group of people, when Jesus stood behind me and put his hand on my shoulder. I've never had another experience like that. It was eye-opening."

My mom's revelation reflects an important vacuum in all of us.

OUR GREATEST NEED IS TO see God.

It's like being an adopted child. You might have grown up in an incredibly loving home with really supportive parents, but many adoptive children have an innate need to see their birth mother; to see the one from whom they came; to see the one they look like, whose DNA they carry.

God didn't need to create the universe or humanity. God was and is complete. Yet here we are. Have you ever wondered why?

YOU AND I WERE CREATED FOR THE PURPOSE OF intimate companionship WITH GOD.

I love the way the first book of the Bible suggests what had been the ideal of man and woman walking with God in the garden. (See Genesis 3:8-9.) It was originally an intimate bond, but notice how soon it fell apart. After they had sinned and broken the relationship, Adam and Eve hid from God. (See Genesis 3:10-21.) In our brokenness, our desire to be self-sufficient, we have each short-circuited the intimacy of that relationship. We need to touch the invisible, but instead we cut ourselves off from the very One we want to see and touch.

ESCAPE FROM CHAOS

When I go skiing, I must escape to the mountains.

The same pattern works for our spirits. We need to escape the chaos.

The urgent will always crowd your life and demand the margins. Even for Jesus, the crowds with their needs were always around him. If he had allowed them to dictate his agenda, he wouldn't have had the focus or energy to do his one thing.

To be empowered as the people God created us to be, we must create boundaries and margins in our lives.

GOD SPEAKS in the margins.

To hear God, we must create spaces. You need to create mountain moments in your day.

Elijah went to the mountain. He experienced an astonishing connection with God on Mount Carmel. (See 1 Kings 19:11-13.) Moses received the Ten Commandments from God at the top of Mount Sinai. (See Exodus 19:16–20:21.) Both Elijah and Moses understood that God speaks in the uncluttered margins. God demonstrated his power in an amazing way through Elijah. But typical of the God-life paradox, Elijah immediately found himself in a season of self-doubt and depression after this great victory.

Have you ever found yourself there? It's up and then down. When Elijah was down, the voice of God came to him and told him, "Go out and stand on the mountain before the Lord, for the Lord is about to pass by" (1 Kings 19:11a).

What happened next? "Now there was a great wind, so strong that it was splitting mountains and breaking rocks in pieces before the Lord, but the Lord was not in the wind; and after the wind an earthquake, but the Lord was not in the earthquake; and after the earthquake a fire, but the Lord was not in the fire; and after the fire a sound of sheer silence. When Elijah heard it, he wrapped his face in his mantle and went out and stood at the entrance of the cave" (1 Kings 19:11b-13a).

GOD WAS IN THE silence,

NOT THE NOISE.

We, too, need to create those spaces, boundaries, and margins in our lives.

WE CAN'T hear God IN THE NOISE.

God speaks out of the "sound" of sheer silence.

ENCOUNTER GOD

When we hear God in the margins and solitude, we begin to form life images. The pictures formed out of our God encounters are important because they give us power, purpose, and direction.

YOUR one thing COMES FROM

YOUR GOD PICTURE.

A person with a God picture has a clear life direction. You become what you look at.

Where are you looking? What are your life pictures?

Moses was a powerful leader. Many of the people who were part of his faith community thought he was irresponsible because he would often escape from the urgent to dream God's dreams. More than once Moses took off for the mountain for an extended period of time. (See Exodus 24:18; 34:28; Deuteronomy 10:10.)

When Moses was away, God spoke to him. Moses formed a picture, wrote it down, drew it on stone, and came down the mountain with it firmly in his grasp. We call that picture the Ten Commandments. We're still living by it. What a powerful life picture!

Contrast Moses' action with what his brother did. Aaron's purpose was also to serve God, but Aaron was constantly engaged with the demands of the people's expectations. He had no time to escape, no margins in his life, and no time for a breather. Because he didn't encounter God or escape the chaos, he went out and crafted an idol. The fruit of his life was well-intentioned idolatry. (See Exodus 32:1-6.)

WHEN WE ENCOUNTER GOD, WE GET OUR RHYTHM BACK.
WE REMEMBER whose we are.

When I go to the top of a mountain, I am amazed by the panoramic view. One time Jonathan and I were skiing in West Virginia. We went to a place on the mountain where we knew there wouldn't be many people. When we got to the top of the lift, we saw five deer coming out of the woods. We also found bear tracks in the snow. What a memorable experience we had that day!

YOU REMEMBER YOUR HEALTHY LIFE PICTURE
WHEN YOU TAKE TIME TO escape the chaos.

The cloud, the presence of God, comes to you. That's what happened to Jesus' disciples when they were on the mountain and touched the mystery of God's presence. (See Luke 9:28-36.)

I was planning a message at Ginghamsburg about escaping the chaos to encounter God. I walked by our graphic designer's desk as he was working on the ski metaphor, using scanned pictures of various ski adventures. "That's my son, Jonathan, in that picture," I commented. He was amazed that I could so quickly identify Jonathan, since the photo was four years old. "I take pictures when I'm on top of the mountain," I explained. "I took that picture."

When we encounter God on the mountain, we take life pictures. They become the maps that direct our energy to the big-picture purpose of God.

Mountaintop experiences can also occur at sea level and indoors. Recently our family had to squeeze into a tiny motel room in Florida. The room was so small that we couldn't open the door when the rollaway was set up. It was a time of creating life margins. Ten years earlier I would have wondered why we were staying in a dump like that, and my stress level would have gone up. Instead, I saw the awe and wonder of my grown family being in the same room, laughing and having a good time.

A week later I was alone in a New Haven, Connecticut, motel. Our worship team had spoken at Yale University. Wiped out, I was asleep before 10:00 p.m. Then at 1:00 a.m., I was wide-awake, staring at the clock. We had to get up at 5:00 a.m. to catch a ride to the airport. I tried to go back to sleep, but the harder I tried, the more awake I became. Instead of thinking of everything that I had to do, I got out my Bible and asked God to meet me. As I reflected on the Word, I listened to God.

I caught my flight home, went directly to my office, and worked through the afternoon and into the evening, having had only a few hours of sleep during the

previous forty-eight hours. I have a tendency to become irritable at those times and emotionally beat up the people around me. But because I had made time to encounter God, I became life-giving, not life-robbing. My time with God reminded me who I was and whose I was.

For us to be complete, happy, and whole people, we have to create those spaces for God to speak in the margins in our lives. A lot of us are running ragged because we're filling up the margins.

If you're a disciple of Jesus and you feel depleted, with nothing left to give, you have to receive before you can give. You need to escape before you can engage.

Solitude COMES BEFORE service.

ENGAGEMENT WITH OTHERS

The top of the mountain, however, is never the final destination. When you reach the top, you're only halfway there. When you go skiing, you go to the top so you can come down. Same with the spiritual world.

As quarterback for the Dallas Cowboys, Troy Aikman led his team to a Superbowl victory. Instead of celebrating the night away with his team, he sat in his room, drank a beer by himself, and felt an overwhelming sense of depression. During his early teenage years, he had thought all his problems would be solved the moment he turned sixteen and was able to buy a car. They weren't. So he looked for a higher mountain to climb. His ambition became to play pro football. The Superbowl win took him to the top of pro football, and he still found himself asking, "Now what?"[1]

When people climb Mount Everest, few fatalities occur on the way up. It seems that death most often happens on the way down. When the climbers reach the summit, they are so awed by the view that they forget it is not the final destination. They still need to make it safely back down. They spend too much time at the top, using up their precious resources and don't have the energy to make it all the way back down.

To FULLY encounter God,

WE CAN'T STAY AT THE TOP.

When Jesus' disciples reached the top, they thought it was a cool place. "We can all hang out here, you can feed us every day, and we'll stay here and enjoy this amazing experience," they expressed to Jesus. (See Matthew 17:4.)

Many followers of Jesus have had powerful experiences with God. The cloud of God's presence comes over us. We sense awe and wonder. We realize that we're in the presence of the living Lord, and yet hours later we find ourselves in the low place of self-doubt and confusion.

Do you remember the enthusiasm you felt at one of those high moments? For some reason, the memory dims over time. It no longer feeds us because the experience was incomplete.

WE hear God ON THE MOUNTAIN, BUT WE see God WHEN WE COME DOWN AND SERVE PEOPLE.

Jesus, after his mountaintop meeting with God, descended the next day. He came down to serve human needs. Jesus modeled that any real God-encounter will lead us to get down and work where people are.

People in our churches are sometimes like the disciples, wanting to stay at the top, wanting more spiritual food. Some people at Ginghamsburg say, "Mike, you don't feed me anymore." Many of these people forget that our connection with God is never complete until we make the commitment to sacrifice our personal needs and come down from the mountains of our personal spiritual journeys to serve the needs of the oppressed and hurting all around us.

Spiritual hunger CAN APPEAR IN MANY DIFFERENT FORMS.

We don't always recognize it as spiritual in nature. It can appear as restlessness; longing; dissatisfaction; and, for many of us, even boredom. The things that offer immediate gratification do not ultimately fill us up. When we're bored we eat, shop, buy a new car, or otherwise engage our consumer mentality. Or we may find a little project to become involved with, never realizing that the hunger pangs rumble from a deeper place in our beings.

Consumer binges or feel-good food can never satisfy the hunger. God alone is the Bread of Life. Only God offers living water and invites us to drink freely.

When you ski, the thrill of coming down makes you realize why you went up in the first place. What happens after you leave the top is what makes you want to do it again.

We follow God not in five easy steps but in the paradox of going up and coming down. As you experience that truth, you will help others experience God in those same ways.

LOOKING FOR JESUS AT EVERY TURN

Jesus told his disciples, "It is to your advantage that I go away, for if I do not go away, the Advocate will not come to you" (John 16:7b). In essence he is saying, "If I go away and God comes in the Spirit, not only will you have God *with* you and *for* you, but you will have God *in* you."

THIS IS THE

most intimate OF ALL RELATIONSHIPS.

Through the Holy Spirit, we can have that intimacy in every dimension of life. In the forty days after the Resurrection, Jesus weaned the disciples from their dependence upon him in the "package" of his body so that they could get to the most intimate of all relationships: his presence through the Spirit. In those forty days, Jesus never appeared in a way in which he was easily recognized. The disciples received only glimpses.

The Apostle Paul explained what happened: "Even though we once knew Christ from a human point of view, we know him no longer in that way" (2 Corinthians 5:16b). Jesus reminded us of the same thing when he said, "I will never leave you or forsake you" (Hebrews 13:5b) and "I am with you always, to the end of the age" (Matthew 28:20b). But a lot of us keep looking to a Jesus who came in a human package. Don't get stuck there.

Easter happened, and so Jesus isn't restricted to the box, that human body you have pictured in your mind.

WE NEED TO BE LOOKING FOR

the resurrected Jesus AT EVERY TURN.

Where do *you* see Jesus? Jesus said, "I'm hungry, and you're going to see me and give me something to eat. I'm sick, and you're going to come and minister to me. I'm in prison, and you're going to visit me." (See Matthew 25.)

One year during Holy Week, Carolyn and I were in Titusville, Florida, with our son's high school baseball team. It was 10:00 at night, and we were in a laundromat in a bad area of town, doing laundry for all twenty-one players. It stunk, but the smell matched the kind of place it was. Bars covered the windows. We were there at our own risk. In the corner sat a street person who appeared not to have all his wits about him. He had taken off his clothes and was washing them in the washer.

I began to look around, and I recognized that laundromat as just the kind of place where Jesus hangs out. These are the people with whom Jesus lives! All of a sudden, it was Holy Week, and I was recognizing the presence of Jesus, and my heart began to sing the music of the risen Christ. I began telling some of the other baseball parents who were there about how God did incredible things by creating each one of us. We were holding church at 10:00 at night in a Titusville laundromat, and Jesus was right there with us, *in* us.

God says, "trust me," not "see me." (See 2 Corinthians 5:7.) Trust is not based on sight. Most of us are like Jesus' disciple Thomas who said, "Unless I see the mark of the nails in his hands, and put my finger in the mark of the nails and my hand in his side, I will not believe" (John 20:25b). Jesus loved Thomas so much that he allowed Thomas to touch him. Sometimes, on very rare occasions, God allows us to have very vivid sensory encounters.

But Jesus reminds us that the eyes of the heart are better: "Jesus said to him, 'Have you believed because you have seen me? Blessed are those who have not seen and yet have come to believe'" (John 20:29). Blessed are those who will believe even though they don't see because they have the most intimate of all relationships. We live by faith ("trust me"), not sight ("see me").

Don't limit your picture of Jesus to the time he walked around for thirty years on earth. God is not limited to that form of Jesus because Jesus is in us in Spirit today.

JESUS NOW LOOKS MORE LIKE

the orphan and widow—

LIKE YOU AND ME.

Identify a healthy life picture that will remind you who you are and whose you are as you serve Jesus through others.

One Church That's UnLearning

Mosaic, downtown Los Angeles, California
www.mosaic.org

QUICK DESCRIPTION: a community that lives by faith, is known by love, and offers a voice of hope.

HISTORY: Southern Baptist; started in 1953. Began at nightclub campus in 1998, began at downtown loft in 2000, began at San Gabriel high school campus in 2001.

ATTENDANCE: 1,200

THEME: Awakening the Spirit of Creativity

WHAT THE LEADER SAYS: "I'm unLearning the way Jesus touches people through people. We give the small things to Jesus, while bringing our bigger issues to Freud. We've lost confidence in Jesus' ability to heal, transform, and make us whole. Jesus is interested in making whole disciples out of broken people.

"God specializes in fixing broken relationships. We were created for the purpose of intimate companionship with him. We lack power and credibility if we offer to others a level of relationship that we don't know in reality ourselves.

"We don't focus on growing the church but on connecting people with the kingdom of God through Jesus. But we are not about church growth; we're about doing the right things. That attitude costs us a lot of growth.

"Our front door is the transformed lives of our people. If you get people in the right environments, where Jesus shows up, their lives will change forever."

—*Erwin McManus, lead pastor, has been a part of Mosaic since 1992; age early forties.*

How Are **you** UnLearning?

• Describe a recent situation in your life in which solitude came before service. What are the implications for your life as a leader?

• What song matches who you are when you are healthy?

• Sketch or make a collage of the healthy life picture of who you are becoming.

ENDNOTES

1. Skip Hollandsworth, "The Real Troy Aikman," Texas Monthly (December 1998).

Pressing Forward Without Looking Back

Once you begin the journey, keep pressing forward.
Lot's wife looked back and became an inanimate part of
her environment. People of faith steer toward the place of
God's promises.

The world is waiting for the reality of God's presence to be demonstrated through you. Your most important priority is to develop the spiritual person within you and then to allow your growth to influence others.

I AM UNLEARNING FAITH AS BEING the absence of doubt. FAITH IS acting on WHAT GOD SAYS.

Faith is acting on God's directive at any given time in spite of what I feel or think. Faith is pressing forward no matter what.

Many of us wish we had more faith. But that's not really what we need; we simply need to act. We simply need to act on the measure of faith that we've already received through God's grace.

People of faith don't look back. Jesus said, "No one who puts a hand to the plow and looks back is fit for the kingdom of God" (Luke 9:62).

The new generation of leaders, like the ancient sages of biblical faith, is looking forward "to the city that has foundations, whose architect and builder is God" (Hebrews 11:10b).

God told Lot to leave the intensely negative environment found in the city of Sodom. Sodom contained no healthy life pictures for Lot's family or for future generations of God's people. (See Genesis 19:15.) If you are hanging out in a place

that lacks healthy life pictures, you'd better get out or you will be destroyed.

God essentially said to Lot, "Once you begin moving toward the place of my promised future, don't look back. Don't stop. Don't be distracted." But Lot's wife looked back. She couldn't let go of familiar habits and defeating behavior patterns that gave her comfort and security. She looked back and became part of her environment. In that wilderness area, when salty water dries up, it leaves salt deposits. Lot's wife literally became what she focused upon. The paralysis of fear from the dysfunction of her past became the reality of her existence.

DISTRACTION FROM OUR GOD PICTURE

I am spiritually challenged by distraction. In my spiritual disability and dysfunction, I can be easily sidetracked.

My friend Ron played an important role in the early formation of my faith when I was a student at the University of Cincinnati. He was a fraternity president. He was aggressive and persistent about Jesus. He was part of a Christian organization on campus, and that's where I met him.

Ron would take me to meetings at various fraternities, and then he'd make me tell how Jesus had come into my life and changed it. I'd be walking across campus with Ron, who was an extrovert, and he'd stop people coming our way, hand them leaflets, and say, "Our organization is having a Campus Life meeting Friday night; we'd love for you to come." Then he'd turn to me and say something like, "This is my friend Mike Slaughter. Mike, why don't you tell them about the difference God has made in your life?" Ron often placed me in these awkward, challenging situations, but I looked up to him for his boldness and sincerity.

One week Ron suddenly disappeared. He didn't come to the Friday night Campus Life meeting or the weekend Bible study. When I didn't see him at the meetings for several weeks, I finally started asking around.

"Didn't you hear about Ron?" one of the leadership team members replied. "His fraternity had a meeting with him and said, 'Ron, you have to make a choice. It's this Jesus thing or the fraternity, but you can't be our president and do both.' "

"What a no-brainer choice," I replied. "The kingdom of God is an easy choice over a fraternity."

Ron had looked back. He traded the kingdom of God for a seduction. He would no longer be with us.

We all suffer from varying degrees of spiritual dysfunction. Even after three years with Jesus, his disciples struggled with doubt, unbelief, guilt, and denial.

Our ability to be faithful, fruitful, and to finish the mission for which we were sent depends largely on one thing: our God picture.

SUBSTITUTING WITH PROPS

A prop is anything we use to create a role other than that which God created for us. Sometimes we work hard to create alternate images. Some of us create images out of what we have: cars, clothes, friends, or the neighborhood in which we live. We'll go into debt to form our images. For others of us, our images come from what we do—from our success, from what we accomplish—rather than from Christ.

Does your image or identity come from what you have? from what you do? or from Christ whom you follow? Do you see the subtle difference?

UnLearning Moment

What is your image? Give one example of how it is increasingly coming from Christ rather than what you have or do.

To go into debt to create a reality is nothing less than a deception. When you need a drink or drug to relax, it's a demonic decoy. When you dress suggestively or inappropriately, guess who your wardrobe designer is? Our props slip into our identities with great subtlety.

Don't trade your God identity for the lure of image.

SMILES ARE PART OF THE PICTURE

I remember the first time I saw the picture *Jesus Laughing*. It was startling at first. I had never seen Jesus portrayed that way. Does radical discipleship have room for silly moments and grins?

Jesus must have smiled and laughed. Not just because some of the things he said were funny. Not just because children were drawn to him. People of Jesus know how to laugh out loud because we're not on earth just to make bread, but to make life—and life has some downright funny moments.

When our children were small, financial necessity dictated that a family dinner out would be at the food court at the local mall. Once when we had just gone through the ritual of choosing dinners from different vendors, Jonathan said, "I gotta potty, Daddy."

The restroom had a little yellow sign in front of the door that said, "Caution Wet Floor." Jon, too young to read it, ran into the bathroom. "Wait a minute," I hollered, but it was too late. As I stepped through the door I saw him sliding, falling on his back, and continuing to travel across the floor. He flew under a stall. A man was sitting there with his pants around his ankles, looking at Jon lying at his feet. I had to reach in under the stall and pull Jon out.

Jon had a dazed look on his face and a knot growing out of his forehead from hitting the bottom of the stall as he slid under it. He had black wet dirt on his clothes from the still unclean floor. What was I going to tell his mother?

We weren't in the restroom four minutes, but when we walked out, the first words I heard were, "What on earth did you do to him?" After Carolyn heard my explanation, we both burst out in laughter.

Oh, the memories!

IF YOU'RE fully present IN THE MOMENT, YOU'LL FIND LAUGHTER IN LIFE.

You'll realize that you are responsible for your own smile. Sometimes we expect those closest to us to be responsible for our emotional attitudes. My smile is not dependent upon how well things are going or if they're not going so well. It comes when, in the spirit of Matthew 6:33, I seek first the immediate presence of God, the activity of God, the intimate connection that God wants to have in the details of my life, and everything else finds its place.

Jesus says life isn't about food, cars, houses, or even our physical pain or emotional stress. It's about seeking first that joyful, immediate presence of God. And everything else will fall into place.

FAILING FORWARD

A group of servants from Ginghamsburg's worship team, working on a video clip for a weekend celebration, went to a place that had an indoor climbing wall. They each tried it and had to confront three fears while climbing: 1) that they would fall; 2) that they would get stuck halfway up, unable to go either up or down; and 3) that they would look stupid.

In the spiritual life, the promise is that you cannot fall. The unfailing love of God is the climbing harness that will not falter. Unfailing love will not give way, will not drop you, and will not break. In our life journey the only secure footing is God's love.

UNFAILING LOVE MEANS | can fail, but I won't fall.

Just as the wall-climbing team learned to "tie on," Jesus' followers learn to tie themselves to the amazing love of God.

WE CAN never MESS UP BADLY ENOUGH TO EXCEED GOD'S CAPACITY TO forgive.

Many of us, when it comes to our relationship with God, feel like we are hanging from a string. Our sense is that God is waiting to snip the string at the first sign of relapse or mess-up. We feel like we are hanging in a precarious, temporary position, based on our ability to be pleasing to God. We feel that if we mess up, there will be no blessing or second chances.

We can totally miss God's promise of unfailing love. When we do, we begin to project onto others the same critical, judgmental attitude that we perceive comes from God. You will truly love others only to the degree that you experience God's love.

A CLEAR LIFE PICTURE AS A LEADER

I can't believe how many people tell me that God doesn't speak to them.

The number one question people ask me when they call or come to my office is "How can I know God's purpose for my life? How do you hear God speak?" You must train yourself to listen to the Holy Spirit.

God is speaking right now. Do you hear what God is saying? You can hear better if you are pressing forward toward the picture of God's promising future.

What have you been thinking about lately? What has been consuming your thoughts? What have you been talking about lately? What have you been spending significant time doing?

You experience your future by your thoughts, words, and actions. Every thought you think, every word you speak, and every action you commit has a long-term consequence. You can be purposeful about creating your future, or you can create your future by default.

If someone asked you in an elevator what you do, what would your twenty-second response be? Mine is "to connect people with their God destiny." The longer version is "to be a source of inspiration and transformation by promoting, advancing, and demonstrating the cause of Jesus Christ in a post-Christian world."

We don't have time to play the kingdom of church. The spiritual godfathers and godmothers of your church might be very happy if you continue doing church the way they've always done it—without any risk or change. But we have time in life to obey only one voice—the voice of God.

Don't settle

FOR ANYTHING LESS THAN GOD'S CREATIVE PURPOSE.

Walt Disney was the visionary behind Orlando's Disney World, but he died before it was built. When it was completed, they held an elaborate grand opening ceremony. The story is told, although it cannot be documented, that someone commented to his widow, "Too bad Walt couldn't have seen this."

Mrs. Disney replied, "Oh, but he did!"

The Apostle Paul said, "I was not disobedient to the heavenly vision." That was his one thing. He saw it. He followed and obeyed one voice.

Moses had a clear life picture. "He persevered as though he saw him who is invisible" (Hebrews 11:27b). When you continually adjust your life picture by the intuitive voice of the invisible, you will stay vital for life. You experience the invisible not through the eyes of your physical body but through the eyes of your heart.

I don't like it that my generation is becoming the early-retirement generation. Jesus didn't die on the golf course. Retirement for many is about material security and leisure. When you have enough stuff, then you can retire. Too many ministers in their early to middle fifties are already talking about their dreams of retirement. What has happened to the power of call?

UnLearning leaders will lead the generation of regeneration. Regeneration is about spirit.

TRUE GREATNESS IS ABOUT YOUR SPIRIT—IT'S

who God is making you to be,

NOT HOW MUCH STUFF YOU HAVE.

Life is about what we are willing to give up for the kingdom of God. You have to lose life to find it. The amount of life that you're willing to give up for God determines the impact you'll have for God's purpose.

One Church That's
UnLearning

Frontline, Vienna, Virginia (just outside Washington, D.C.)
www.frontline.to or www.mcleanbible.org

QUICK DESCRIPTION: Frontline is a ministry of McLean Bible Church that uniquely targets people in the 18-35 age group. Through worship, small groups, activities, and Bible studies, Frontline seeks to present the gospel of Jesus Christ in a relevant, authentic fashion. Frontline is actively involved in serving throughout the community through various service projects and has a thriving short-term missions program. During 2001 at least sixteen teams went out to various locations throughout the world.

HISTORY: nondenominational; McLean Bible Church started in 1961, Frontline started in 1994.

ATTENDANCE: 1,800 in two Sunday-evening services

THEME: True Greatness

WHAT THE LEADER SAYS: "I'm unLearning that people need to see their pastor as having it 'all together.' It seems the older generations don't really want to know that their leaders have feet of clay, but the younger generations know they do—and they want to hear them admit it. When we share our pain in the context of a sermon or lesson, and when we take off our own masks and let people inside, it endears them to us as well as increases our credibility. Transparency and authenticity are extremely valuable in communicating the grace and love of Jesus Christ.

"None of us can make it alone. I think the younger generations realize this more than ever and are willing to take off the facade of rugged individualism and reach out to others for community."

—Ken Baugh, pastor to Frontline at McLean Bible Church, and Associate Senior Pastor of McLean Bible Church; age mid-thirties.

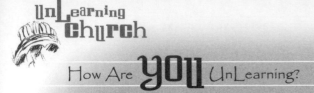

How Are **you** UnLearning?

- Describe the picture you see of God's promise for your life. How are you looking beyond things in this life that hold or distract you?

- What are the implications of your life picture for your leadership in the church?

A Theology of Sweat

Outreach goes way beyond bringing somebody to church. UnLearners engage in human need. They do all they can, give all they can, and serve all they can until everyone gets to the table of God.

God didn't come to temples or palaces but to broken people.

In an encounter Jesus had with his disciple Peter after the Resurrection, he asked Peter the same thing three times: "Do you love me?" (John 21:15-17). Each time Peter said "yes," and each time Jesus told him to do the same thing: "Feed my sheep."

Jesus' preoccupation is with people who have need. He is concerned about those who are still on the outside and are not yet experiencing God's party. "If you love me," he is saying, "you will be my connection to those who are not here."

Jesus says that if you want to experience God, you have to be serving people.

UNLEARNING CHURCHES ARE SERVICE COMMUNITIES THAT EMPOWER PEOPLE TO engage human need IN THE WORLD.

These leaders personally demonstrate the kind of authentic faith that embodies involvement with the lost and oppressed.

I am unLearning the kind of lifestyle that would allow me to go home from church meetings oblivious to lost and hurting people all around me.

DON'T EAT 'TIL EVERYONE'S AT THE TABLE

One of the images Jesus often used for the community of God's people was that of a dinner party. In several places the New Testament writers describe a fantastic party, a banquet to top all banquets, put on by God. Anyone knows that if you are going to a dinner party, you need to be aware of certain principles of etiquette.

The first basic principle is that you don't eat until everyone is at the table.

The night before our daughter, Kristen, graduated from college, our son, Jonathan, had his next-to-final baseball game. I went to the game, and then he and I drove through the night to get to Kristen's graduation. We arrived about 3:00 a.m. and crashed in bed. When we got up, we didn't have time for breakfast because we had to get to the graduation early enough to find prime seats for taking pictures. After the graduation, we congratulated Kristen's friends and then moved Kristen out of her apartment. By the time we finished, it was late afternoon, and we still hadn't eaten. I was bordering on being famished. We had invited sixteen family members and friends who were making the journey to the graduation to celebrate the special occasion with us over dinner. We drove to the restaurant and had to wait for all sixteen people to get there. The food finally started coming, but not everyone's came at the same time. Mine came out first, so I cheated a little on my etiquette. When no one was looking, I'd grab a little piece of food with my fingers and put it in my mouth.

Do we as Jesus' followers do the same thing? As children we learned at home that you don't eat until everyone is at the table. Yet we come to this wonderful spiritual "banquet" of God, and we start scrambling for the best seats. We fight for the best parking spots. We crowd ahead of others in the coffee line.

WE MISS the heart of God,

WHICH IS FOCUSED ON THOSE WHO AREN'T YET AT THE TABLE.

The biblical story, from Genesis to Revelation, describes God's pursuit of those who are lost.

The only other place (besides his question to Peter) where Jesus makes the same point three times in a row is Luke 15. He tells three parables of lost things, all with the same point: Lost people matter to God.

"Which one of you, having a hundred sheep and losing one of them, does not leave the ninety-nine in the wilderness and go after the one that is lost until he finds it?" asks Jesus (Luke 15:4). Does your heart feel complete when ninety-nine are in the house, or have you saved energy, effort, a good seat, and the best parking spot for the one who's still on the outside?

I once did an hour of book signings but went away discouraged. A long line of people made me feel like I had a fan club: "Oh, Mike, you are so successful. You've had the opportunity to experience the growth of a large church. You should feel so satisfied."

"Why do I still feel a sense of incompleteness?" I wondered. "It's true I have seen God work in incredible ways through Carolyn's and my ministry." But I certainly didn't feel successful.

I'm beginning to realize why: I'm unLearning success and learning how to be more connected with God's heart. As long as one person is on the outside, God grieves. If you are connected to God, you grieve with God.

We have some close relatives who are precious people but make it to church only about twice a year. Every time we sit down to prayerfully plan worship at Ginghamsburg, I think, "Is this something that would be appetizing to them?" I also think about all the kids I coached in baseball through the years: "Will what we're doing connect with them?"

What does it mean to love God? I don't want to eat until everyone is at the table.

UnLearning Moment

Who do you know and care about who is not yet a regular guest at God's table?

DON'T PULL THE CHAIR OUT FROM UNDER PEOPLE

The first time I got spanked in school—it was in fourth grade—I had pulled the chair out from under a classmate. I learned the hard way that you don't do that. The same is true in church.

Jesus welcomed all people. Sometimes our manner communicates, "I love you but until you get your act together, you are sort of a second-class citizen. I will tolerate you, but you are really a source of disappointment." We welcome with our words, but we belittle with our actions and church structures. We pull the chair out.

God welcomes us, and it's certainly not because we're worthy to receive divine grace. Jesus' parable of a prodigal son (see Luke 15:11-32) is about the teen who grows up in a God-centered home with all of the graces for life and success.

His family can't believe that he's their son when he announces at Christmas break that he's not going back for his second semester. "I need to find myself and have a little life," he says. He decides to travel through Europe during the next months, and he spends all his college money on the wrong kind of things. He begins to experiment with things that soon become addictions. His infrequent

prayers are really worries about the possibilities of contracting a sexually transmitted disease.

Things get worse, and he comes to a point where he doesn't even know how to get back home. Yet as someone created for relationship, he longs for his father's love.

Here's the whole point of Jesus' story: Long before the young man gets his act together, and while he is still a long way off from where he needs to be, the father goes running toward him. Not only does he pursue his son, but when he finds him, he quickly forgives and embraces him. The father is willing to get his son's stench on his own clothes!

I am a part of the church of Jesus Christ because when I was a teenager, Carolyn and her boyfriend at that time invited me to go with them to their youth group. They demonstrated God's enthusiastic welcome. This was a time when a whole lot of mothers wouldn't let me date their daughters. (I certainly wouldn't let my daughter date me the way I was!)

God does not love us because we are loveable, DESERVING, OR HAVE OUR ACTS TOGETHER.

God loves us because it is the nature of a good parent to do so.

I recall a time early in my ministry when, as a young preacher, I still wore a suit on Sunday mornings. Three-piece suits and three-month-old babies are not a great combination. One Sunday morning we got our baby, Kristen, changed and ready to go to church when, somehow, she pooped on my suit. I'm sure we had put the diapers on right, but the mess got through. I changed into my only other suit, picked her back up, and she did it again!

I'd like to say that was the last time, but my sweet, beautiful Kristen continued to poop on me in different ways throughout the years (parents will know exactly what I am talking about). But I'm her dad, so not only do I love her dearly, but my desire is to make her feel welcome with me, even on hard-to-love days.

I recently noticed a poster in a store window about a little girl in my community who has been missing for over a year. I stopped and thought about the relentless, inexhaustible, consuming, not-giving-up love of her mother and father. That's the nature of what it means to be a parent.

Jesus says to you and me, "Love as I have loved you. Show that same love to others. Not people you respect—the loveable and righteous. Welcome the non-respected, the undesirable, and the unloving. Don't pull the chair out."

WHEN YOU HAVE BEEN invaded by the presence of God,

YOU HAVE ONE PURPOSE IN THE WORLD:

TO BE A WITNESS OF JESUS CHRIST.

Jesus said the Holy Spirit empowers us as his witnesses in our neighborhoods, communities, and beyond, even to the ends of the earth. (See Acts 1:8.)

A lot of people in the church today confuse witnessing with an attitude of "God told me to tell you..." Being a witness and trying to speak for God are not the same thing. There is a fine line between the two. So many times we try to tell other people the will of God for their lives, and we end up pulling out the chair. That's not the kind of leadership that Jesus modeled.

YOU HAVE TO SWEAT IN THE KITCHEN

If there is going to be a dinner party, somebody has to sweat in the kitchen. Ross Dillahunt, a member at Ginghamsburg for the last fifteen years, practices a *sweat theology*. He understands Jesus' question, "Ross, do you love me?" because he works to find connection points to people who are not here.

Ross has experienced the importance of being invited. "Fifteen years ago," he says, "John Thomas invited me to a men's dinner. Ohio Congressman Tony Hall was the speaker, and I made a recommitment to Christ after hearing his talk."

A few years ago, Ross thought the Lord wanted him to start something at the car dealership where he works. As he explains, "We started a Bible study there, and I kept inviting the guys to come, but the only ones showing up were those who were already Christians—and there weren't very many of them! So we changed the format a little and decided to have a men's breakfast in the conference room of the dealership. Now, once a month, we bring in a Christian speaker who shares a personal story or a message. My wife cooks the breakfast, and the salesmen show up." Ross and Pam Dillahunt know the literal value of sweat equity in the kitchen—especially Pam, Ross emphasizes.

Ross also reaches beyond his immediate circle of relationships. One day as he was driving to an Optimist Club meeting he sensed the Lord prompting him to stop and speak about Jesus to a certain tattered-looking man sitting on the side of the road. "I knew that the Lord wanted me to do this because my stomach feels pressure whenever God wants me to do something. My hands start getting clammy. I didn't really want to stop. I wanted to get to the meeting on time, but

I knew that I was supposed to go back. So I turned around, and I told this man that Jesus loved him, that God had a plan for his life, and that God had not given up on him. I prayed with him before I left. He did not make a life change right then, but he thanked me for stopping." Who knows what God might still do in that man's life, and Ross' sharing might have been the start of it.

We need to bring more people than others think possible, welcome more people than others think wise, and serve more people than others think practical. We must do for love what we thought impossible before. That is the lifestyle of a Jesus follower.

One Church That's UnLearning

Lutheran Church of Hope, West Des Moines, Iowa
www.hopewdm.org

QUICK DESCRIPTION: To reach out to the world around us and share the everlasting love of Jesus Christ, becoming a Spirited, growing, and Christ-centered community filled with hope.

HISTORY: Evangelical Lutheran Church in America (ELCA); started 1950, restarted 1994.

ATTENDANCE: three thousand in six services: two Saturday evenings, three Sunday mornings, and one Sunday evening

THEME: Inviting All Ages to One Table

WHAT THE LEADER SAYS: "Our congregation has become rather intergenerational without much effort. About three years ago we tried to do a 'Gen-X' service, got about three hundred people to attend, and then were promptly told by those three hundred people that they wanted to worship with people who were different than themselves. Our response was to do a very counterintuitive thing and mix the postmoderns with the moderns. It has been well received so far.

"Our mission statement affirms that we are a church of individuals, different in many ways, yet called together by God to be one in ministry and mission. We like unchurched people, and we know what a difference Jesus can make in their lives. For this reason we seek to reach out to the world around us and share the everlasting love of Jesus Christ, even through our worship.

—Richard Webb, teaching pastor, has been with the church since 2000; age early thirties.

How Are **you** UnLearning?

• What inhibitions about radical love are you unLearning?

• How does your lifestyle demonstrate a wild and determined commitment to show divine love to others?

㉑
Full-Term Faith

"The things I do, you will do, and greater than this, you will do" (Jesus). Keep your eyes focused on Jesus and persevere. Your mission is the fulfillment of Jesus' mission in the world.

Full-term faith is the confidence that no matter how ordinary or quiet my life is, God is going to work a miracle through it to touch the world.

I AM UNLEARNING THE ATTITUDE

THAT ETERNAL LIFE IS MERELY THE PROMISE THAT I WILL live forever.

Endless eternity could get very boring without the enduring quality that comes from a vital relationship with Jesus.

The while-on-earth implications of eternal life are significant. It begins now, as Jesus said, "Whoever believes *has* eternal life" (John 6:47b, emphasis added). When you and I accept eternal life, we receive the character of God, the life of Jesus, and the love of Jesus now. As those who have "become participants of the divine nature" (2 Peter 1:4b), we begin demonstrating God's life and love to those around us.

That's what our baptism communicates. Baptism is fearless identification with Jesus Christ. It says we have devoted ourselves to relationship in Christ and through Christian community.

FOR THE CHRISTIAN,
Jesus IS THE
BEGINNING, MIDDLE, AND END OF OUR EXISTENCE.

When Jesus lives through us by the Holy Spirit, we do what Jesus is doing, we go where Jesus is going, and we speak what Jesus is speaking. "This is eternal life, that they may know you, the only true God, and Jesus Christ whom you have sent" (John 17:3).

We are not here on this planet to make a name for ourselves. We are here as stewards of God's enterprises.

An entrepreneur is somebody who is creative in building a business. We exist to be spiritual entrepreneurs who carry out the business of God. Only what we do for the benefit of God and the benefit of others will live beyond us. We're not here to be self-entrepreneurs.

Jesus sends us out to do his mission. "As the Father has sent me, so I send you," Jesus says (John 20:21b). He sends us to carry out the enterprises of God.

An ancient Christian tradition offers an image of God sending every person into the world with a special message to deliver. One person has a special song to sing to others, and another has a special act of love to give. No one else can speak my message, sing my song, or offer my act of love. Jesus sends us out for the business of God, for the purpose of God.

In the movie *Pay It Forward*, a young boy came up with a big, hairy, audacious goal to change the world. His idea was to have every person influence three other people by an act of service and kindness. The assistance would be something they couldn't do for themselves. The three people who received help would then "pay it forward" by influencing three other people.

Jesus' plan is similar. We change the world by serving one person at a time, influencing one person at a time, and connecting one person at a time to God.

Our mission is the continuation of Jesus' mission in the world. It is doable. Jesus said, "The one who believes in me will also do the works that I do and, in fact, will do greater works than these" (John 14:12). Don't miss the implications of these words!

This promise opens new windows on our life missions. Doing "greater works" than even Jesus did gives us the assurance that when we leave planet Earth, the Holy Spirit will have conceived and given birth to God's purpose through our life energies.

Postmodern people are looking for authenticity. They do not seek explanations about God so much as authentic life-demonstration of biblical relevance.

UnLearning leaders
ARE MORE ABOUT A DEMONSTRATION OF A GREATER-WORKS-THAN-THESE, authentic faith THAN ABOUT SIMPLISTIC JESUS SLOGANS AND MAGIC FAITH FORMULAS.

Their greatest persuasion point is authentic life experience, not argumentative reasoning.

BUILDING A RELATIONSHIP

I have an autographed baseball that reads, "To Mike, Pete Rose." I have one of Pete Rose's baseball bats that he used during the 1970s. I can tell you Pete Rose's batting averages and his all-time hit total. My family was in the stadium the night he made his most famous hit. I know all about Pete Rose, but I have never met him.

Just as knowing about Pete Rose doesn't mean I have a relationship with him, for many Christian leaders, knowledge *about* God doesn't mean they *know* God. In fact, sometimes our knowledge of God gets in the way of knowing God.

A relationship is an interchange of love and thought. More than knowledge alone, it involves intimacy. The parallel is true in our experience with Jesus. In the early church, "they devoted themselves to the apostles' teaching and fellowship, to the breaking of bread and the prayers" (Acts 2:42). A relationship involves work. It is an investment.

When Carolyn and I got married, I thought, "Wow, now we are married. We will be close."

Carolyn had a different idea. She wanted to start going to marriage enrichment seminars and marriage classes. She wanted us to listen to tapes. She would say, "Mike, the church is having a Dobson film series on marriage. Let's go." She would leave subtle hints, such as books on my nightstand.

"We don't have to do all that stuff to be close. We just need to be married," I said.

It took me years, but I discovered that she is right. We now devote ourselves to growing together. It involves ongoing, sustained effort.

Reading the Bible is like receiving love letters from my wife. I pay very close attention. I reflect on the words.

I begin each day in an interchange of love and thought with God. Sometimes when I listen to God through the Scripture, a message comes over me like the impact of a love letter. We can too easily forget the intimate, unrelenting, passionate love that Jesus has for us. He is passionately in love with us! The most core truth of the universe is "Jesus loves me, this I know." Jesus did not sign his message as "Profoundly, your God," but "To Mike, with love."

DEVELOPING A SENSE OF MISSION READINESS

In January of 1995, I was coming back home late one evening on a plane from Chicago when the oxygen masks suddenly dropped. The plane depressurized and went into a forty-second controlled dive. The pilot pulled out at eight thousand feet. We found out later that part of the cargo door had blown off. When he told us that we could take off the masks, he said, "I'm going to try to make it back to Chicago. I don't know what happened, but if I can't make it back, I'll tell you where I'll try to land the plane."

What a feeling when those masks popped out! It sounded like an air gun or a BB rifle. I thought, "There is a good chance I'm not going to make it back. This isn't how I planned it." My other thought was: "There is no door out of this kind of situation. I have no way out."

Death usually comes unannounced. One hundred percent of us will die sooner or later.

We cannot cheat death, so there is only one way to live.

WE ARE TO LIVE IN A CONSTANT STATE OF mission readiness.

Jesus said we are to be watchful, to "be like those who are waiting for their master to return from the wedding banquet, so that they may open the door for him as soon as he comes and knocks" (Luke 12:36).

UnLearning Moment

Reflect on your sense of mission readiness. State the one thing you're most ready for God to do through your day-to-day life.

When our family goes to a movie, one of the children might have a bag of popcorn, candy, or cookies. I sometimes think I'd like just a couple of munches. So I put my hand out. My son's response is "Dad! Get your own." But I don't want a whole bag. I want only a couple of cookies!

Where did he get the cookies in the first place? From me, right? So I put my hand out again, and I give him a hard look. "Give me some cookies!" He offers me one. "I want more than one." Jonathan explains that he has only *eight* left.

All of us do likewise. We become accustomed to focusing on our little bag. We protect it. We ration its contents. As we grow older, we learn more sophisticated approaches. But when we die, all that's left is an empty little bag.

Life is a lot more than our little bag of Famous Amos cookies. It is about mission, impact, and destiny. It's not about *my* cookies but cookies for the world. I want to leave more behind than little empty cookie bags.

Psalm 84:11b says, "No good thing does the Lord withhold from those who walk uprightly." God's blessings are not limited. If I go through life focused only on my

little cookie bag, I am focused on limitations. I begin to live out of fear. I lose sleep, and I lose creative energy. I start to live out of a mindset of scarcity. I learn to hoard.

This bag is only the container. It is not the source of the blessing. The eight cookies in the bag are not all there is. Plenty more are available at the Famous Amos factory. Where did Jonathan get the resources to purchase the cookies in the first place? From his father's hand!

Fear and scarcity are the opposite of faith and trust. We serve a generous God who blesses us without limitation. The Apostle Paul said that God "by the power at work within us is able to accomplish abundantly far more than all we can ask or imagine" (Ephesians 3:20). When we believe God and act on God's promise, the outcome is always greater than the expectation.

Mary, the mother of Jesus, said, "Every generation is going to call me blessed." (See Luke 1:48.) For Mary, the statement did not come from ego. She had eyes to see that God was birthing greatness through her life. Sight and vision are not the same thing. When your eyes are open, you are able to name God's miracle. When the angel gave God's message to Mary, she didn't say, "No, not me! Take my cousin; use her! I'm too busy right now. Wait for a less busy time in my life." She affirmed, "Here I am."

Blessed are the ones who believe that what the Lord tells them will happen will indeed happen! These are people who bet their lives on what God says. They don't merely believe in God. Believing is easy and costs nothing. They have full-term faith.

To Mary, the angel's message meant more than a pregnancy. God was going to birth a miracle through her! From that time on, what God would do through her ordinary life would touch every human being. That's the difference between just believing in God and having full-term faith.

SOWING WISELY, REAPING GREATLY

God wants us to be involved. When some of us pray, we say, "Oh, Lord, help my relationship with my spouse to be intimate and deep." Then we sit back and wonder why it doesn't happen by next week. We fail to plant the seeds God gives us. Remember, we reap what we sow.

The same principle works in raising our children and in our business ventures. Everything is about investment and partnership with God. "Whoever sows sparingly will also reap sparingly, and whoever sows generously will also reap generously" (2 Corinthians 9:6, NIV).

A farmer and his friend were standing by a field of ripe wheat, which was ready to harvest. The friend looked at the farmer and said, "Doesn't God do a marvelous job?" The farmer replied, "You should have seen the field when God had it by himself!"

God doesn't work alone. God is in the seed business. In our consumer mentality, we expect God to give us fully ripened fruit, but more often God's mission is a partnership of investment that depends on you and me. As the Apostle Paul said, "I planted, Apollos watered, but God gave the growth" (1 Corinthians 3:6).

Second Corinthians 9:10 says, "He who supplies seed to the sower and bread for food will supply and multiply your seed for sowing and increase the harvest of your righteousness." This is a great biblical principle. The more I invest in God's purpose, the more God will entrust blessings to me. This practice is critical to Christian living.

When I came to Ginghamsburg, we did one worship celebration a weekend. For 116 years this had been a single-celebration congregation. I thought that since you reap what you sow, *why not do two?* After two I thought, "Let's do three." One night I was driving home after coaching my son in little league baseball, and I passed the Catholic church with a full parking lot on a Saturday evening. I thought, "Why not do Saturday evenings?"

Jesus says that when the Spirit comes into our lives, rivers of living water shall flow from our innermost being. (See John 7:38.) We will be blessings to other people. That's what I am as a follower of Jesus and as a leader of other followers. I serve as a channel to pass God's blessings through myself to others. And I will reap what I sow.

We were created to be a blessing. Jesus says, "Give, and it will be given to you. A good measure, pressed down, shaken together, running over, will be put into your lap; for the measure you give will be the measure you get back" (Luke 6:38).

How do we receive blessings from God? Keep all we have? Guard the bag? No, we give, and it will be given to us.

How many cookies will I give you? Take the bag! The measure I give will be the measure I get back.

FOLLOWING THE HEART OF GOD

A giving attitude represents the heart of God. It is why Jesus said we would do greater things than he did.

WE ARE NOT HERE TO BE

consumers; WE'RE HERE TO BE

conceivers.

We are to become pregnant and then to give birth to God's purpose.

Chances are you've barely begun to break ground in your life on what God can accomplish through the Holy Spirit. But you're never too old. Moses was eighty years old before he committed himself to the unplowed ground. Look what God did through him, leading the children of Israel out of Pharaoh's domination, across the desert, and to the Promised Land.

It's time to break up your unplowed ground, your unrealized potential in the Holy Spirit. When you act on God's promise, the outcome will always be greater than your expectation. What a God!

Your mission IS AS CRITICAL AS THE MISSION OF JESUS.

Your unique gift is critical to God's mission and purpose. You are created and called for the purpose of serving with your gifts, giving your life regardless of the cost.

The ultimate turn-around moment in my life came when I was nineteen years old. For the first time, I discovered that God wanted to use me—right where I lived, with the gifts God had given me. I didn't need to travel to some far-off place; I was to be who God created me to be right here in my neighborhood. This is what it means to be a follower of Jesus.

LETTING GOD GIVE THROUGH YOU

Jesus, on his way to Jerusalem on the Sunday morning of the last week of his earthly life, met two blind beggars. They didn't understand what Jesus was about to go through. They yelled out something to the effect of, "Jesus, Jesus, do you have anything left to give us?" It's amazing that Jesus was spiritually and emotionally available to stop and give himself for those folks. "Moved with compassion, Jesus touched their eyes. Immediately they regained their sight and followed him" (Matthew 20:34).

As a leader, do you ever feel you have nothing left to give? One night I was sitting in my house, having just returned from a trip out of town. It was the night before Ash Wednesday, which is a big day at Ginghamsburg, and I was exhausted. The doorbell rang at 9:20 p.m. I said, "Who could possibly be at the door this late?"

I opened the door, and it was a senior in college whom Carolyn and I have sponsored on missionary trips. He was planning to spend a year on a mission in China. He wanted to talk. Inside I felt, "I don't feel like talking," but we welcomed him and heard his request for monthly support.

I felt like saying, "Go away!" But the secret of Christian life is not living out of what we feel but out of what we know and have experienced to be true.

WE HAVE received GENEROUSLY,

AND SO WE CAN give GENEROUSLY.

I ask you a very serious question: Are you available to God and available to others?

Shortly before his arrest in the garden, Jesus was sweating blood as he prayed. He was the only person to be born who never sinned, but yet he was going to receive all the hell that you and I deserve. He was preparing to face a punishment that you and I will never know, because of what he did.

During those tumultuous hours, he prayed, "Not my will but yours be done" (Luke 22:42b).

LIFE IS ABOUT LIVING available to God.

Is there anything in your life that is keeping you from being totally available to God?

Full-term faith is not about your convenience. Full-term faith is about giving birth to God's miracle in you. It's about saying to God, "I am yours. Take my life, God, for your purpose and your pleasure."

One Church That's UnLearning

The Village Church, Greenwich Village, Manhattan, New York
www.villagechurchnyc.com

QUICK DESCRIPTION: A church eager to see Greenwich Village become a place where Jesus Christ is known, honored, and served.

HISTORY: Presbyterian Church in America; started in 1994.

WORSHIP ATTENDANCE: 250 in one Sunday-morning service

THEME: Continuing Jesus' Mission in the World

WHAT THE LEADER SAYS: "If Jesus were living here in Greenwich Village, New York City's most prominent homosexual community, what would he be doing? For The Village Church, this simple question led to a radical unLearning: We should have a ministry to people with AIDS. So we created i58, based on Isaiah 58:10-11 as our guiding Scripture. We cook and serve food to more than one hundred people with AIDS biweekly, including New York's oldest AIDS residents. Showing concern to a physically and spiritually broken community has also opened doors to share the gospel. More than one person has commented, 'I've noticed a big difference in your volunteers—you actually care about people. You don't treat us like charity cases,' and 'Our clients want you back.' "

—*Ron Koustas, leader of the Isaiah 58 Project since 1994; age early forties.*

How Are you UnLearning?

• Make that last sentence your prayer: "I am yours. Take my life, God, for your purpose and your pleasure." How is God answering it?

• Talk about your faith journey. What are you unLearning as you grow toward full-term faith?

From Eyes Wide Shut to Arms Wide Open

The identity of a Jesus-follower is found in service. If you love God, you can't help but serve God. We are never more like God than when we become the hands and feet of Jesus, poised to serve the needs of others.

Jesus modeled a life of service to others. By beginning each day in relationship with his Father and listening to the Father's instructions, he knew how, when, and who to serve.

Jesus made time to go and listen to God. "In the morning, while it was still very dark, he got up and went out to a deserted place, and there he prayed" (Mark 1:35). He learned what makes God's heart cry.

Then he went out and found people who were hurting and in need. "And he went throughout Galilee, proclaiming the message in their synagogues and casting out demons" (Mark 1:39).

One of the first people he came across was a leper who desperately wanted Jesus to make him well. Motivated by the heart of God, Jesus chose to be involved. Full of compassion, Jesus stretched out his hand to the leper, broke social convention by touching him, and said, "I do choose. Be made clean!" (Mark 1:41b).

JESUS LOVES LEPERS; WE PREFER LEATHER

Who are today's lepers? They are the people we won't touch.

Our daughter needed a fall jacket, so our family went to the mall. As we walked into Eddie Bauer, I noticed a nice three-hundred-dollar men's black leather jacket.

Until I had this sensory experience, I hadn't thought about needing a new coat. Now, all of a sudden, the urge hit me.

Our daughter, well discipled by her mother's example, said, "Dad, you've got a black leather jacket already."

"Yes, but it's from 1986," I heard myself reply. "And it's gathered in the back. The new ones are straight."

I didn't buy the jacket, but I struggle with the spirit of consumerism. I fight it all the time. I still find myself wanting that jacket! Is my focus on leather jackets or on the heart of God?

WE LIKE THE TOUCH OF leather, BUT JESUS WANTS US TO TOUCH THE lepers.

On an airplane trip, my seat assignment happened to be next to a woman named Karen Fisher. She used to be part of Ginghamsburg before moving to Colorado. "You know when my life was changed?" she asked. Karen reminisced that in 1988 a Ginghamsburg mission pastor invited her to go with a team to New York City. "My life has never been the same," she said. "I determined to go to college and then to work with kids. That's what I'm doing now."

Our son, Jonathan, also goes to New York City with Ginghamsburg teams. They work with alcoholics, drug addicts, and homeless people in the Bowery section of Manhattan. He's in college now, but he keeps telling us, "When I start making money, it's going to be for the homeless poor." The experience of coming into contact with hurting people and serving them has changed him in ways that months of small group Bible study alone cannot.

WHEN WE SERVE, WE SEE the heart of God.

When we die, God isn't going to ask us how stylish our jackets were or what style of music we preferred in church. I don't believe God deeply cares whether we use hymnals or video projection.

God is going to ask WHAT YOU AND I DID WITH THE POOR AND HURTING!

What is true religion? The Bible says it is "to care for orphans and widows in their distress, and to keep oneself unstained by the world" (James 1:27b).

UnLearning Moment

What question are you prepared for God to ask you when you enter heaven? What are you unLearning about the kinds of questions God tends to ask?

To be Christ-like means to become decreasingly self-centered and increasingly concerned about the needs of those around us.

WE ARE NOT HERE ON EARTH TO BUILD SANCTUARIES OF BELIEF BUT
armies of action.

Jesus didn't stop with contemplating his beliefs. He became intimately involved in the lives of other people. That's the example his followers are to follow. James 4:7a says "Submit yourselves therefore to God." That means to act on what we already believe.

Evil's temptation is subtle. Evil will tempt us to be "just a little less": a little less than honest, a little less than loving, or a little less than good. Every day I have to work hard to resist being "a little less" than what God wants—a little less compassionate, a little less involved.

Evil tempts me to read the news headlines about human suffering and do nothing more than say, "Isn't it a shame?" When I align myself with the heart of God, I will resist evil and do more than express emotional feelings. I am to commit my resources, with arms wide open, to do something about it.

The psalmist said, "Those who go out weeping, *bearing the seed for sowing*"—with action to match intention—"shall come home with shouts of joy, carrying their sheaves" (Psalm 126:6, emphasis added).

PEOPLE WHO WENT TO THE NEED

Tom and Elaine Sampley were part of the foundational group during my first years at Ginghamsburg. They lived on a lovely spread, complete with horses. Inside their house, just off their master bedroom, was a bathroom as big as my family room. It featured a sunken whirlpool tub that could seat six. The corner of the bathroom had a Swedish sauna. You could spend all day being pampered in their home! We have many great memories of Tom and Elaine's parties.

In 1988 the Sampleys transitioned from a safe, predictable lifestyle to a life path of involvement with causes that touch the heart of God. They sold their

home, went to a Bible school, and now serve as missionaries in the Czech Republic. Tom's income as a real estate broker was significantly more than the $1,250 they currently make each month. They've long since used up their savings.

What cry of their heart led them to do such a wild and crazy thing? "Through the teaching we heard at church and from our personal reading of God's Word," Tom explained,

"WE DECIDED THAT

commitment without action

IS NOT TOTAL COMMITMENT."

"God moved us away and gave us assurance in our hearts: 'You don't know where you're going yet, but I do. And I'll be with you each step of the way.' "

The Sampleys' research indicates that only two out of every one thousand people in the Czech Republic claim any allegiance to Jesus Christ. "God grew us to the point where we were willing to take what we had learned to people who haven't had as many opportunities to hear it as freely as we have here in the States," Tom said.

Tom and Elaine together teach an hour of English and an hour of Bible. They offer these classes several times a week. They use the Bible as their textbook for the English training. "It's really awesome to see the Word penetrate the hearts of these atheistic people," says Elaine. "We combine the school with a coffeehouse ministry."

Tom talked one night with Jiri (pronounced YEAR-jee), a young man who claimed that the Bible is outdated and irrelevant for today. He claimed to have no interest in God. Yet Jiri was so hungry spiritually that they talked for more than an hour. "Is this overwhelming you, Jiri?" Tom asked at one point. "Do we need to quit here?"

"No, tell me more," Jiri replied. By this time Jiri was on the edge of his seat. Clearly the Holy Spirit was quickening his interest.

After the animated conversation had continued for some time, Tom said to Jiri, "Do you want to accept Jesus? Do you want to make that commitment in your life?"

"Yes," Jiri replied.

Jiri joined a church and became part of a Bible study. As he stood firm for Jesus, he began to challenge others, "Why don't you come to believe?" Jiri has become a follower of Jesus who is reproducing himself in others.

The Sampleys are unLearning life as they follow Jesus' voice into a fearless future. They are my heroes. "They're real, live-action God heroes," I tell the children of our church.

"THIS IS as big as it gets."
THE SAMPLEYS REPRESENT KINGDOM SUCCESS.

They are the model of what we're trying to reproduce at Ginghamsburg.

THE INSULATION OF CHURCH LITE

One reason I admire the Sampleys is that they don't close their eyes or arms to the kind of need that confronts them each day in the Czech Republic.

I find it easy to block it out. Carolyn and I were watching television after working hard one day. The program was about children with cancer. It was gut-wrenching. We looked at each other and said, "Enough is enough." We turned off the show.

Isn't that easy to do? We build insulated cocoons to protect ourselves.

WE END UP LIVING WITH eyes wide shut.

If everything feels OK around me, I'm oblivious to the pain of people outside my insulated boundaries. We end up developing a narrow, superficial, selfish sense of well-being.

One way I deal with stress is through humor. As a kid, I was the family comedian. When things got bad at school, I'd work especially hard at home on my comedy routines. More than once, when my clowning at home became extreme, my dad told my mom, "You'd better call the principal because obviously he's failing something again."

I was the epitome of superficial, my masking laughter motivated by denial. This is what Jesus means when he says to people who follow him, in effect, "You have eyes to see, but you don't see. And you have ears to hear, but you're not getting it." (See Matthew 13:16-23.) You are guarding yourself well. You're oblivious to God and to the needs of others.

As a result, we do church lite. We enjoy awesome music, we sing songs from the heart, we study the Bible with passion, and we tell our stories. We feel inspired as a result. We go out oblivious to lost and hurting people all around us. As the prophet observed in Isaiah 58, we go through all the right religious motions, but we're blinded to the needs around us. We laugh and have a sense of security.

WE FEEL GOOD, BUT

God is not laughing.

We might change the channel, but God doesn't. As James 5:1-6 and other passages teach, God hears the cries of people we don't hear. God hears the cries of the people we've hurt, oppressed, and cut out of the abundance we experience. They might be as close as our own home or neighbors in our community.

"Lament and mourn and weep. Let your laughter be turned into mourning and your joy into dejection" (James 4:9). We are to align our hearts with God's heart. We are to cry about the things God cries about.

God seeks

THAT WHICH IS LOST AND

restores THAT WHICH IS BROKEN.

Do I personally grieve with God? Does my heart grieve until the purpose of God is fulfilled? Does this attitude permeate my leadership in Christ's church?

After reading this passage in James, I picked up Newsweek magazine and saw photos from the winter of 1998-1999 in the former Soviet Union. I saw a little boy sleeping in a sewer. Everything about me wanted to change the channel, as I had done with Carolyn at home because it is easy for me to be a jerk. I want to live in my protected bubble.

Instead, we figured out a way to act on it as a church.

Years ago, during the Ethiopian food crisis, we had led a multiple-week challenge to sponsor children through World Vision. The response was powerful. The people of Ginghamsburg adopted more than 260 children. To this day my wife and I still sponsor a needy overseas child.

I brought the same child sponsorship idea back in the fall of 2000. Our people staffed a display table in our church lobby for two weeks so that each household in our church would seriously consider giving about twenty-five dollars a month to feed children, clothe a child, and offer medical care. This action step is so simple, but it is neglected by many Christians. We worship Jesus not just through the words we sing, but also by our simple actions to the "least" of these: "Truly I tell you, just as you did it to one of the least of these who are members of my family, you did it to me" (Matthew 25:40).

MORE THAN MONEY

Giving is good, but we must lead our people to do more than give money. More important is their personal involvement of time and energy. In a typical year, a dozen or so teams go out from Ginghamsburg on mission, financing it out of their own resources. We've sent several of those teams to help build the John Perkins house in Jackson, Mississippi. Our New Path Ministry deals with housing for single moms here in our community. Jim Taylor, who runs a Ford dealership nearby, sponsors hot lunches for the homeless. Louella Thompson, supported financially and assisted by many Ginghamsburg small groups, feeds the hungry daily in nearby Middletown, Ohio.

The youth of our church have another way of opening their arms to others. Back in 1989 one of Ginghamsburg's teens went on a mission trip, became inspired for service, and came back wanting to do something on an ongoing basis. He took his bicycle to Dayton and started riding around the Parkside project section, getting to know some of the neighborhood kids. His passion increased, and he got more teens involved.

As relationships with these kids started to form, Clubhouse grew. Some two hundred teenagers now give one or more afternoons a week to touch these kids' lives. They run a ministry called Clubhouse in the inner city of Dayton and throughout the Miami valley, working with at-risk kids in remedial math, reading, faith-based teachings, sports, and arts. Over the years Clubhouse has empowered over nine hundred teens to go out and do local ministry. They have started Clubhouses in Cincinnati and more recently at Miami University in Oxford, Ohio. There are also five teen-initiated Clubhouses in South Carolina.

Clubhouse is more than tutoring and racial reconciliation. The mission of Clubhouse is to train and equip teens to go out and be the hands and feet of Jesus in neighborhoods where a lot of adults probably wouldn't go. According to Cheryl Bender, longtime director of Clubhouse, "These neighborhood kids are discipled. What happens is like our adult discipleship groups or our home groups. These kids become attached to our teens. Many have come to a faith relationship with Jesus Christ."

Today we are making a difference in Jesus' name for children across the United States.

DECIDING TO PAY THE PRICE

What's in the headlines today? As I write this, Arab Palestinians and Israelis, both from the same long-ago father, Abraham, are fighting each other. Christians in

Colombia and Indonesia are abandoning their homes and possessions, fleeing for their lives from people intent on killing them because of their faith. Earthquakes and killer monsoons are wreaking havoc, adding thousands of people to the tens of millions who go to bed hungry and cold each night. Right here in the United States, children die each day from hunger and other poverty-related causes.

My tendency is to live in Mike Slaughter's little shell of isolation. I have to work hard every day first to listen to God, and then to go into God's day serving with my arms wide open.

It's easy to insulate oneself and do church lite. It takes effort to expose myself to the sufferings, needs, and hurts of others, and then to respond wholeheartedly.

The only way we can reflect the heart and concern of God is to follow the admonition of James: "Draw near to God, and he will draw near to you. Cleanse your hands, you sinners, and purify your hearts, you double-minded" (James 4:8).

I start each day with a shower, but one cleansing doesn't usually suffice. My physical body has a tendency to collect dirt as I go through the day. So does my spirit. Selfishness and greed cling to me like dirt! I have to continually practice God's cleansing. It begins with my time alone with God. That is where I get honest with God about my mixed priorities. That is where God begins again to cleanse and transform me.

That same church lite can happen when we're together in Christian community. At church we have a good time and sing great songs, sometimes forgetting that people are lost and in trouble. Jesus taught that the good shepherd will "leave the ninety-nine in the wilderness and go after the one that is lost until he finds it" (Luke 15:4b).

The good shepherd GETS UP AND GOES OUT AFTER THE ONE IN NEED.

How about you? What will you give up to go after that one?

WHAT ARE YOU willing to risk? WHAT IS THE PRICE YOU'RE willing to pay? WHAT PART OF YOUR TIME OR WEALTH ARE YOU willing to commit?

Jesus still cares about the lepers all around us. He serves them through people like you and me.

Committing yourself to the real business of Jesus means going beyond the business of the church.

YOUR SUCCESS WILL BE MEASURED IN

transformed lives,

NOT NUMBERS ON THE CHURCH ROSTER.

One Church That's UnLearning

New Life Fellowship, Elmhurst, New York

QUICK DESCRIPTION: Our mission is setting people free. We exist to glorify God by leading people to a personal relationship with Jesus and by demonstrating the love of Christ across racial, cultural, economic, and gender barriers. Our aim is to equip every member to a) grow in love and devotion to Jesus, b) live in authentic biblical relationships, c) mature in Christ-likeness by working through personal issues, and d) serve with their spiritual gifts and talents to fulfill God's unique calling inside and outside the church. We are committed to training leaders who will plant new churches both in New York City and other urban centers around the world.

HISTORY: affiliated with the Christian & Missionary Alliance; started 1987.

ATTENDANCE: 1,650 in five congregations (two more in progress)

THEME: Learning to Love Well

WHAT THE LEADER SAYS: "I am unLearning to serve God out of duty and learning to serve him out of joy and delight. During the first seven years of pastoring, we were growing, planting congregations, and adding people to God's kingdom. The bad news was that my heart for God and people was slowly shrinking. More important, my wife, the one person to whom I had vowed to love well the rest of my life, felt unvalued. She felt like a single mom. I was too busy and overloaded to have energy for her and our children. My focus was on results, effectiveness, and growth.

"Through sheer grace from God, I began to see that I was saving the whole world and losing my own soul (Matthew 16:26). A gradual but dramatic personal transformation followed in my personal life, marriage, and family. I then led the church through the same journey.

"I firmly believe that God's greatest call for us as leaders is to love him, ourselves, and others well. Paul argues that that is *the* criteria for success. This path to emotional health has been painful and required a great deal of unLearning. The joy and fruit, however, have been inestimable!"

—*Pete Scazzero, lead pastor, has been with the church from the start; age mid-forties.*

How Are YOU UnLearning?

• Jesus' business was to go around opening people's eyes to give them the vision of God. What do you have to unLearn to join him in that mission?

• How will you unLearn these things in your present context?

conclusion

nLearning means going in new directions. It requires following fresh winds of the Holy Spirit. UnLearning leads you to new places where God is moving.

What happens when unLearning churches, unLearning leaders, and unLearning lifestyles converge in one place? YOU SEE faithful communities THAT ARE EFFECTIVELY reaching unchurched populations FOR JESUS CHRIST IN A POSTMODERN, POST-CHRISTIAN WORLD.

Each local expression is distinct. Yet the smell of the same God hovers over them all.

In the business world, when you achieve success you often become important, visible, or famous. We tend to mimic that in the church—judging our success by whether we have a better place at the table, more fame, and more fortune than we did last year.

UnLearning leaders are willing to forsake that kind of success and accomplishment to live in the shadows so that God can work through them. Like Moses, we may not achieve the place of promise in our lifetime, but that's not the issue.

WHAT MATTERS IS THAT God lives large THROUGH OUR LIVES.

Radical church is hard. In my years of following Jesus, I've never known one year to go by without painful struggles. I would prefer a life of ease, but Jesus didn't talk about being comfortable.

Most churches are full of parents and grandparents who are willing to die for their children. But some of us aren't willing to give up music styles or worship styles to reach this next generation. IT'S not the big things THAT WILL STOP THE KINGDOM OF GOD, but the little ones.

To get bigger sometimes means we might have to get smaller. Many of Jesus' disciples walked away when they encountered the cost.

Start empowering a group of people who want to radically demonstrate the love of Jesus Christ in your world.

Start by unLearning.

God is doing a new thing with an emerging generation of leaders and church.

Be there.

appendix
Deeper Impact Samples

Deeper Impact is a resource for individual and group study. It follows up the sermon each week. The biggest use is in the church's small groups, but many individuals use it during the week for their own personal devotions. The following is an example. For further information see www.ginghamsburg.org or phone (937) 667-1069.

LEAVING A LEGACY: 1 Chronicles 28:20

In what way are you "just like" your dad or mom?

Silently read 1 Chronicles 28. Pay special attention to verses 8-9 and 20. Then discuss the following:
- What did you learn about David as a king?

- What did you learn about David as a father?

From the following Scriptures, what influence did David's life have on his children?
- 2 Samuel 11:2-5 and 1 Kings 11:1-3 (Solomon)

- 2 Samuel 11:14-17 and 2 Samuel 13:23-29 (Absalom)

Read 2 Kings 17:40 and discuss these questions.
- What did your parents do that you catch yourself doing?

- What did your parents do that you swore you would never do?

- What did your parents do that you are thankful has been built into your life?

Examine the legacy you'll leave.
- What plan do you have to connect relationally with each of your children?

- How are you intentionally building character in your children? What are the key values you want to see reproduced?

- How will you drive the mission of Jesus forward in your home?

- What is one thing you can do this week to strengthen the promises you've made to your family?

A FOLLOWER'S LIFE: Hebrews 13:7

When you were little, at whom did you look and say, "I want to be just like them"?

Read Acts 18:1-4 and 18-28. Priscilla and Aquila had someone who taught them and someone they taught.
- What does their story say to you about your network of relationships and their purpose in your life?

Read Romans 1:8-13 to discover insights into the relationship between Paul and the believers in Rome.
- What was that relationship like?

- How did Paul encourage their faith development? (9-10)

- What was the intended result? (11)

- We become whom we watch. What people have played a similar role in your life? What part of your life have they influenced?

Each of us needs a dream team of mentors that will help us develop and be significant in God's plan.
- What qualities would you look for in a mentor? What makes a good mentor?

- Who are the people currently leading you in different areas of your development?

- What part does each person play?

God gives something to each of us that others need. We are to release that to others.
- Where are you giving? Of whose dream team are you part?

- In what area of life do you influence others?

- If you are not currently in a mentoring relationship, what steps will you take this week to recruit your dream team?

- Who will you seek out to mentor you? Who will you seek out to mentor?

Take time this week to show your appreciation and thankfulness in some way to those who have been part of your faith development.